"This is indeed a radical book; [...] is-sues it pursues. At the same tin [...] v-ing the real values of our Catho [...] ut as living truths that confront us [...] all the conclusions of the author but we cannot help but be deeply touched by the beautiful and authentic lifesongs. This is a book with which it is well worth spending time."

M. Basil Pennington, O.C.S.O.
Monk of St. Joseph's Abbey, Spencer, MA

"Repeating the lyrical, penetrating style that has become his trademark, Huebsch's latest offering confronts the realities of ordinary human living. He does this within the context of a penetrating critique of the contemporary ethos of the institutional church. All readers may not fully accept his critique, but few will remain untouched by the depth and power of his lifesongs, which will certainly disturb while they enrich. Huebsch's presentation will prove uncomfortable for many. But so have the writings of other Catholic radicals who have also spoken from the fringes of the institutional church. *A Radical Guide* takes us back to the roots of Christianity—the Gospel—in a thoroughly modern setting."

John T. Pawlikowski, O.S.M., Ph.D.
Professor of Social Ethics
Catholic Theological Union

"Bill Huebsch's book is dangerously good: faith-filled but pushing to the edges of faith, honest about church and honest about compassion, poetic but hard-hitting, a survivor's guide for those trapped in the liberal/conservative dead-end. This kind of Catholicity will endure precisely because it is truly Gospel and truly catholic."

Rev. Richard Rohr, O.F.M.
Center for Action and Contemplation

"True to the original meaning of radical, Bill Huebsch traces the roots of how we make right choices in seeking to live whole and holy lives. *A Radical Guide for Catholics* offers a framework of fundamental principles for making moral decisions, which he applies to *our* life stories. He encourages us to trust our truth and share our stories and so create communities of conscience, conviction, and care. These 'lifesongs' are our stories—often poignant, always prayerful, and filled with the passion and promise."

Joseph Nassal, C.PP.S.
Retreat Director

"Bill Huebsch's reflections on the thorny and emotional issues facing Catholics today are a rich source for discernment. They breathe the spirit of compassion and urgency of the message of Jesus. They are marked by a deep understanding of the human person in the struggles for fidelity to the self and to the Lord in the best of the 'Catholic' tradition.

"Everyone will find their own songs reflected in these deeply moving meditations. We are especially pleased to see the experiences of gay and lesbian Catholics playing a role among these voices. Their testimonies, so often silenced, neglected, or discounted, will broaden the appeal of this book and make it inclusive in the fullest sense of being 'catholic.'"

Robert Nugent, S.D.S.
Jeannine Gramick, S.S.N.T.
Co-Authors, *Building Bridges: Gay & Lesbian Reality
and the Catholic Church*

"Bill Huebsch has done it again! He has blessed us with a book that nourishes the human spirit, celebrates our inmost and private moments of pain, struggle, and joy, and causes the heart to soar. It is a must read. This book is a delight and a treasure for all Catholics who take their spiritual odyssey seriously.

"Huebsch beautifully portrays what the Catholic psyche has been experiencing for the past three decades. By putting this into words, he has written a book that has the power to heal the inner self as we stormily approach the third millennium of the Christian era."

Dick Westley
Loyola University of Chicago
Author of *Good Things Happen:
Experiencing Community in Small Groups*

"The author takes some of the most pressing and painful questions of our time for those who would live as faithful Catholics, and handles them with wisdom, boldness, and wit."

Carolyn Osiek, R.S.C.J.
Catholic Theological Union

# a RADICAL* GUIDE for CATHOLICS

**\*** rooted in
the essentials
of our faith

BILL HUEBSCH
*with David Peterson*

TWENTY-THIRD PUBLICATIONS
Mystic, Connecticut 06355

Twenty-Third Publications
185 Willow Street
P.O. Box 180
Mystic CT 06355
(203) 536-2611
800-321-0411

ISBN 0-89622-525-9
Library of Congress Catalog Card Number 92-81719

# Preface

## Acknowledging My Co-Conspirators

To conspire with someone is, literally, to "breathe together" with him or her. It is to share one breathe, one spirit, one vision, and one quest. The ones with whom we conspire in life are the ones whose guiding questions lead us, the ones whose lives are lived with an honesty and openness that challenge us, the ones whose stories are normative for us. They are the ones with whom we share a common spirit.

I have such conspirators, many of them yet unknown to me. They are the ones whose stories I'm telling here. They're the women and men who stand at the center, and sometimes at the edge, of the church—or even outside its official doors! They're the men and women struggling to hear their conscience, learning to trust what they hear, and courageous enough to live according to that trust. This book is for them, really, and they are its authors. I am only their spokesperson.

There are other conspirators, too. David Peterson, whose work helped accomplish this project, is certainly one. David is a free-lance writer and poet who lives in Minneapolis, Minnesota. He has worked with me throughout this project, writing and editing alongside me. His poetic touch is evident throughout this book, especially in some of the LifeSongs. David, too, has his own conspirators. Chief among them is Brother Dan Korn who has been his mentor and friend. It was Dan who taught David to be an honest follower of Christ, to really live in the Light, to become Christ for others.

Another conspirator of mine is Tom Smyth of New York who first called me to freedom, who first filled me with hope and a glimpse of what could be. Ken Schmitz and Judy Jackson, therapists and spiritual directors in St. Paul, Minnesota, are others for me. Their spirit fills this project and their insights have so often become my own that it's hard for me to separate where our "breathing together" starts and stops.

CathyAnn Beaty is also a conspirator with me. She is co-pastor of a congregation of the United Church of Christ in Minneapolis, one that is open and affirming. In a sense, she is really *my* pastor. Without doubt, she is the religious leader who has had the most influence in my spiritual life in the past year. Like a compass, she has pointed me in the direction of the Heart of the Gospels. It was with her that I had my "first experience of a woman" as a pastor.

Fran Ferder and John Heagle, therapists and theologians in Seattle, Washington, have shown me spirit and energy, kindness and heart. They have demonstrated the Gospel to me in such a way that when they speak, I no longer hear only their words but I hear *a life lived in fidelity*, the deepest sort of fidelity. We have breathed together deeply, both with laughter and tears, and we go on sharing that "fresh breeze" together.

One day a couple years ago my phone rang and the caller entered my life with a force (and almost a vengence!) that has made us conspirators of the highest order: Richard Groves of Portland, Oregon, the author and one of the producers of the *Desales* program for adult formation and now *Inneraction*, which has the same mission. Richard and Mary Groves and their entire team at Morningstar Productions in Portland are part of this conspiracy.

During the Persian Gulf War in 1991 when I knew I needed to speak to someone whose voice would be a stable one, calling for justice and peace with clarity, I called Joe Nassal in Kansas City, Missouri. We hardly needed to speak at all, so close was our breathing together about that war. As I marched off in my first protest against the killing, Joe marched with me.

And, of course, this list would be incomplete without those whom I have never met but whose willingness to risk everything in the search for truth has led me here: Carol Gilligan, Charles Curran, Leonardo Boff, Matthew Fox, Rosemary Radford Ruether, and others. And those whom I do know: Carolyn Osiek, Michael Crosby, Margo LaBert, and others.

I must add, very importantly, two other conspirators: Neil and Pat Kluepfel at Twenty-Third Publications in Mystic, Connecticut, where this book is made available to you. Their commitment to the work of the Spirit is a model to others.

# Contents

## LifeSongs

## Part Four
# Women

## Reflection

## LifeSongs

## Part Five
# Gay or Lesbian Christians

## Reflections

## LifeSongs

## Part Six
# Money and the Modern Catholic

# a RADICAL* GUIDE for CATHOLICS

# Introduction

At first glance, some readers may think this guide will make it easier to be Catholic.

Nothing could be further from the truth.

This book will make it more challenging to be radically Catholic, which is to say "rooted" in the essentials of our faith, because it urges us to take more seriously our common call to follow our conscience. That's not an easy task; only those in touch with their roots will have the courage and insight to do so.

So don't be fooled. For many of us, this guide won't make it easier to be Catholic Christians; it will make it much more difficult. It's always more difficult to be in touch with one's roots, to be radical.

It would be easier to blindly and obligingly follow the rules. It would be easier to ignore the questions altogether and live unthinkingly. It would be easier to write off those with whom you disagree about moral questions and "do your own thing." None of that is recommended in this guide.

This guide urges us to face today's moral and lifestyle questions—and ourselves with them. It urges us to come face to face with each other in communities of conscience, to do so openly and honestly, and then to *live* accordingly. The dreams and visions formed in such communities will surely change the world! It urges us to move from a private vision of life, a private set of decisions made in isolation, to a *shared* vision.

It won't be easy to do this. But many of us are ready to begin.

Deeply rooted Catholics are beginning again to "form" the church, rather than simply "join" it. A new paradigm of church is current today, one in which we take seriously the teachings of the Second Vatican Council that "the church is the People of God...."

This new paradigm is a great challenge to Catholics today and calls for us all to be deeply in touch with God's presence within and among us.

This book is a guide to help the birth of that new paradigm of church.

For a very long time, we've been institutionalized: a fixed, predictable church where compassion and conscience-formation took a back seat to law and order. We've been a church with a primary focus on organizing parishes, selecting bishops, disciplining those who disagree with official teaching, and worrying about the decline in "vocations." We've even allowed ourselves to wander into silly arguments over altar bread recipes!

The church, even in its institutional form, has been a gift to the world in many, many ways. It has often spoken the truth courageously and firmly when others looked the other way. It has provided a home for many on their spiritual journey. It has been served by pastors and bishops who opened their doors to integration, to the poor, to refugees, and to others when most in the culture preferred not to see them.

But it has also become entrenched at times. Like an unwatched bull whose horn grows into the side of its skull and renders it insane, the church has allowed itself to become compromised in the dominant culture. And it has failed to see its own faults here, failed to recognize its own inner dysfunction. Our own physical plant has made it necessary for us to spend large sums on maintainance rather than on the work of Matthew 25. Our own clerical system has begun to restrict available leadership. And our own insistence on following rules has sometimes failed to develop sensitive Catholic consciences.

The most seriously harmful outcome of this institutional approach, however, has been that we've deprived the church of eucharist. We pack parishioners by the thousands into mega, arena-shaped church buildings where sustaining a celebration requires professional actors rather than pastors. Some of the priests we send into the field are without the aptitude or personality for their work, often disemboweling the parishes to which they are assigned. We are petty about who can serve at the altar, who can preach, and who can receive communion. And in the worst cases, we have actually preferred to cancel eucharist rather than widen our view of ministry!

Listen to us: we would *cancel* eucharist before we'd accept a married, female, or partnered gay or lesbian presider! Good grief! When will enough be enough?

But today a new spirit is blowing in the church and it's one we've only begun to recognize and understand. Today we are learning how to "form" the church in order to "trans-form" the world. We are learning to see ourselves as church, the New Community that Jesus envisioned, washing the feet of the world.

We're unfamiliar with taking charge, however, with choosing our own leaders, with making community decisions in a democratic yet prophetic structure. We're unfamiliar with taking bread and wine into our own hands, unfamiliar with taking responsibility for moral decisions about how we'll live in the modern world and how we'll do that together as church. We're unfamiliar with "breaking open the Word" and, because we are, we're also unfamiliar with its power!

And, most importantly, we've had such a strong focus for so long on the inner life of the church—its needs and problems—that we've forgotten our real mission: to transform the world. We've sometimes become incestuous, breeding off one another and failing to be the seed of new life for the world.

We will form the New Community of Jesus when we step forward and take charge of that task ourselves. There's no need to wait for anyone else; we're the ones called—woman or man, Jew or Greek, slave or free—it doesn't matter. In Christ we become One for this task. But this is a new approach for us, a paradigm shift. Instead of waiting for others, it's time to get to work ourselves.

We've often been content to sit back and complain about what others, principally members of the hierarchy, have done or not done. But these men, too, are in this paradigm shift. These men, too, listen to the Spirit in their lives. Many are courageous pastors and teachers of the faith, paying close attention to the presence of the Spirit in the communities to which they're assigned. We're waiting for them to act, perhaps, and they're waiting for us.

The key thing to remember about paradigm shifts in places like the church is that they have their own impetus, their own unfolding power. They aren't anyone's responsibility but rather belong to all of us. That such a shift is needed now is no one's "fault," but if such a shift is not occurring as we would like, the fault can only be our own for failing to take it into our own shared hands.

As Ted Ross, the Jesuit historian, has often said, such a paradigm shift means only that the approach or solution that worked well in one age has now become a burden on the next.

This book offers two important tools for this shifting paradigm of church. First, it offers Reflections on conscience formation and the discernment related to how we live in these modern times. These reflections show great respect for church teaching and seek to balance that with Sacred Scripture and actual human experience.

They do what their name implies: they *reflect* church teaching, Sacred Scripture, and life. They're a mirror into which we can look to find ourselves and our own life stories, which is the second thing this guide offers: LifeSongs. This second offering is something else we badly need: stories of the struggle to live on the margins of the church—or even at its center—with decisions that challenge the old paradigm and sometimes challenge what are still the "official teachings" of the church.

What is our experience like? What have we learned about forming small communities? What's it like for us to choose leaders, to practice radical hospitality, to give away our wealth? How can we become more inclusive, more pluralistic? What have we learned about Christian discernment surrounding the moral questions of today: about birth control, in vitro fertilization, genetic research, divorce and remarriage, gay and lesbian unions, disproportionate wealth, violence to women, and all of it! What happens for us when we celebrate eucharist together in our households and communities? What happens when we don't?

Some of these stories are disturbing, others are poignant, all are real and normative for us today. We call these stories LifeSongs because that's really what they are. Like the psalms of ancient Israel, the canticles and hymns of those touched by God, or the erotic love poems of the Song of Songs, these are a modern story of God's presence and action in our lives.

They are LifeSongs of people in exile, people in captivity, people chosen or rejected, people troubled or at peace. They are the LifeSongs of folks in the center of church life—or at its margins and shadows—LifeSongs of sinners and LifeSongs of saints.

So many people today are alienated from the church. So many feel treated like children, mistrusted with important moral decisions. For so many, as Leonardo Boff has said, the church has been destroyed as home...and has been "turned into a boarding house without the warmth of a great dream, dreamed in community." This guide calls us to dream together, to be at home with one another, to become church again, to own and be the New Community of Jesus.

In writing this, I've struggled with how radical this call to the New Community of Jesus is. I'm a modern person and I resist giving up individualism, resist opening my home to others, resist being a public witness to my conscience. It would be so much easier to hide. In my work on this project I have alternated among tears, laughter, silence, and awe.

I've feared to reach some of my conclusions because I know some people will reject this out-of-hand. Others will reject me. Parts of the new paradigm of church which this Guide represents are not very "Roman" and I'm aware of that. I don't expect Rome to be happy with this, but I hope Rome will listen to the stories of faith this guide presents. These are normative, guiding stories. Encountering them challenged me very much.

David Peterson, the poet working with me, has struggled, too. Both of us have put down the pen and said to the other, "I don't think I want to face this in myself." We have both felt as we did this work that we might have been better off not to have come this far. To encounter the Gospel's call to a radically shared life in the New Community of Jesus has forced us to examine our own lives and choices carefully. It has forced us to study the issues of modern Christian living, to share our questions with others, to share them with each other in our homes, and to change our lives where we have fallen short.

For so long it's been easy to simply go to church and remain a Christian with no radical leanings at all. Now we have begun to really live and share the Gospel. That's radical.

So this hasn't been an easy book to write and I doubt it will be easy to read, if you take it seriously. I encourage you to enter into these questions of conscience, make them your own, go to the Scriptures, read church teaching, share them with your "community," whether it's a formal or informal gathering.

And I encourage you to pray. Above all, to pray. Listen to God speaking to you in the midst of your own life, in your conscience. Trust what you hear. Take time every day for this, in the morning or evening, while driving, in the shower, working in the yard, around the house, on the job: whenever and as often as you can. Make it a habit to "pray always," reflecting and ruminating on the Word as it is proclaimed in your midst.

I hope this guide will lead you to form church, to take charge of your life, and to trust the Voice of the Living God.

Part One

# Conscience

# The Necessity of Intentionally Forming One's Conscience

Our consciences are our deepest inner sanctuaries
        where we find our truest selves.
They are that place
        where God reveals
                our destiny and purpose,
                our most private self,
                our divine legacy.
They are the place
        where church teaching
        meets our own human experience
                to dialogue
                debate
                and decide.
Here is where culture plays out its influence
        along with the arts,
                our companions,
                and the earth as well
                in a grand symphony of Self-in-God.
Here is where God speaks
        most clearly and distinctly,
                because our conscience
                is the place where the divine voice
                        defines us.
The unique Word each of us is,
        the single word God wishes to speak
                to the world through us,
                is articulated in the conscience
                      of each.
Our conscience is the place
        where we are,
                therefore,

ultimately,
most alone.
Not even those we love most,
those who see the greatest part
of our hidden lives,
can know our conscience for us.
This is our sanctuary
where we go alone to pray.
This is where our private rituals
mix with those of church and culture
to reveal Grace.
Grace, after all,
can be seen as a loving energy
which comes from God alone
and which makes it possible for us
to become all we're created to be.
Grace is realized and accepted
in the conscience,
in the willingness to let be
what the divine force desires
for us.
Conscience is formed within us
by listening intently for grace
in prayer
alone time
quiet walks
meditation
spiritual reading
quiet conversation
pillow talk
kitchen table sharing
or many other ways.

And what do we listen intently to hear?
What forms us?
What forms our conscience?

In forming one's conscience,
church rules
stand next to other factors
and play an essential,
though not domineering,
role.

Rather than dominating
　　　the conscience-forming process,
　　　church teaching should help
　　　　　to guide and ground it.
Church rules are,
　　　after all,
　　　really the collected wisdom
　　　　　of the community.
They are our shared
　　　lessons-already-learned.
At their best,
　　　they can be a guide
　　　against which
　　　　　we reflect our own experience,
　　　　　asking how we match up
　　　　　with the rest of the community.


At times we will find ourselves
　　　in tension
　　　with church teaching.
We will find our own conscience
　　　may lead us to decisions and actions
　　　which challenge everything we've known before,
　　　　　including church teaching.
At those times,
　　　we are bound to follow our conscience first
　　　and the failure to do so
　　　　　is a very serious matter for us.
Church teachings develop over time.
　　　They represent wisdom
　　　　　which comes from God alone,
　　　　　directing and forming us
　　　　　for life in these days.
They come from God
　　　through the ordinary lives
　　　　　of individual people,
　　　　　listening to their own
　　　　　　　inner voices of truth
　　　　　and comparing them
　　　　　to the conventional wisdom
　　　　　　　of the church community.
And they come from Sacred Scripture,
　　　constantly new,

constantly informing us again
of the teachings of Jesus.
God's revelation comes through
those of other religious traditions as well:
Native peoples
Muslims
Jews
Buddhists
Hindus
and countless others....
And it comes from you and me
when we honestly speak
from our convictions
even when those convictions
appear to contradict tradition.


Thus the Holy Spirit
continues to guide the church.


Church teaching is one part
of what we consult
in the formation of Christian conscience.
A second source of revelation for us
is Sacred Scripture.
Both the Hebrew
and the Christian Scriptures
are a deep spiritual well
from which we can draw
insight and guidance
abundantly.
But they aren't a "rule book."
We will be tempted to use them
as a source of simple
and absolute
answers,
just as we do Canon Law.
We will be tempted
to go to the Scriptures and ask,
"What does it say here about Divorce?
Or what does it say about Birth Control?
Or Nuclear Bombs?
Or Homosexuality?"
But the stories

of the Hebrew people,
      our Kings and Prophets,
      our Songs of lamentation,
          love,
          or life
are meant to form us
in what it means to know God,
to help us identify
the experience of this God
      in our lives.
They're God's word,
      a word that leads us
          gently
      and does not push us into submission.
The Gospels and letters
      of the Christian people
      are equally forming.
Here the stories help us to know
      how God behaves toward us.
They are powerful sources
      of the Divine Word
      in our lives
          but they don't provide
          a blueprint for life.

For example,
      when a group of folks
      came along one day,
          dragging after them
          a woman who'd broken the rules
      and asking Jesus to condemn her,
      how did he respond?
He asked them to look
      into their own lives,
      to consider their own hearts:
          "Are you without sin?" he asked.
          "Are you so able to condemn?"
He asked them to look into their own hearts
      for this answer
      but he gave no further lectures
          about the rules.
Whether it was rules
      about the Sabaath

or about dining with sinners,
or touching a leper or a corpse,
or following norms for purification,
    he seemed equally cavalier
    about the literal law
    and more concerned
    that the inner lives
        of those around him
        be formed into love.

Reading and reflecting
    on these stories
    of our heritage
        can lead us to deep insights
        about our own lives
        and the decisions we must make there.

Let's pause to review
    a little about what we've said
    so far.
Taking church rules into account
    we have said,
    is one factor
        when forming our consciences.
Sacred Scripture is a second great gift,
    a wonderful source of wisdom,
    an opening into God's heart,
        which taken into prayer
        can produce wonderful fruit
            in conscience formation.

Now, moving on,
    a third factor,
        is intuition.
This is the inner voice,
    the place where we hear ourselves
        feel and think.
It's a "sense" we get
    without always understanding
    where it comes from.
Intuitions are sometimes called
    insights
    or imaginings.

They're the place
        where conscience becomes articulate:
        the place where church teaching,
                sacred scripture,
                and our own experience
                        come together.
In a sense,
        we *know what is right*
        when we trust them.
But we haven't been taught
        to trust our intuitions.
In fact,
        when our intuitions are in tension
        or outright disagreement
                with church teaching
                we've been taught to *mis*trust them.
How do we choose
        when our hearts tell us one thing
        and the rules tell us another?
How do we know what's right
        when our conscience seems to lead us
        in a direction opposite that
                which is the church rule?
It will never be easy
        to sort this out
        but one helpful way to begin
        is with our spiritual companions,
                the fourth factor
                in conscience formation.
Our companions are
        the trusted ones
        with whom we walk in community,
                the ones with whom
                we share meals and leisure time.
In fact,
        the word "companion" means, literally,
        "the one with whom I break bread."
"Talking over the kitchen table"
        with friends and family
        as we sort through church rules,
                scriptural insights,
                and our own experience
                        is crucial.

We know the ones we can go to
      when it's time to sort
      light from dark
         in a life situation that matters.
We know them
      as ones who will tell us the truth,
      ones who have suffered themselves,
         who have managed to follow their own path.
These are the ones among us
      who stand out as friends
      who will say the hard thing,
         love with toughness
         insist on integrity.
These are ones who are committed
      to us doing that, too.
These aren't teachers
      who teach only "what we want to hear"
      but persons who speak for God,
         which is what the word
         "prophet" means.
Such companions are prophets for us
      and for our church.
They help us hear
      what we cannot
         or will not
         hear ourselves.


We all need such companions
      to help sort through
      the "stuff" of life.
It doesn't matter our particular place
      or questions
      or issues.
It doesn't matter whether we're priest,
      or teacher
      or pope,
         the plain truth is
         we do not discern in isolation.
Maybe we're people wondering
      how to possibly make a choice
      when the options all seem difficult,
         when sorting or discerning
         seems impossible.

Maybe we're people
      whose life experience
      doesn't match exactly
            the church's model
            or the culture's.
Maybe our marriage has become violent,
      coercive,
      abusive,
      filled with infidelity
            or is unholy in other ways.
Maybe our sensitivity to the world's poor
      seems to call us
      to work for justice.
Or maybe our wealth has finally gotten to us
      but we don't know how to change,
      how to divest ourselves
            in order to embrace the Gospel
            more fully.
Maybe we're lonely
      or angry
      or hurt
      or displaced.
Maybe we're HIV+
      or dying from AIDS
      or filled with cancer
            or have Alzheimers,
            or other diseases.
Maybe we're facing life from a childhood
      that was filled with horror and violence
      and we cannot find peace as adults.
Maybe we're leaving religious vows
      the priesthood,
      or even the church itself.
Maybe we hear only silence
      when we listen for God
      and have come to the point where we cannot
            bear it any longer.
Or maybe we're simply slumped
      into indifference,
      a dull routine of life which we hate.
Maybe nothing has excited us,
      aroused us,
      or stimulated us in many years

but now we want to feel life fully again
and we don't know how.
Maybe we've finally come to terms
with being gay or lesbian
and know the closet doors must open
despite the rejection
we will feel from
family
culture
and church.
Maybe we're differently abled
or suffering from stroke
or have simply lost abilities
others consider normal.
Maybe a thousand things,
a thousand life experiences
in which sorting through the intuitions
requires a companion.

To sum it up, then,
we form conscience
by "consulting"
Scripture,
our own Intuitions,
Official Church Teachings,
and our Companions.

At its best,
the church provides us
with what we need
to form conscience this way.
It clearly articulates
traditional teachings,
telling stories of others' experiences,
and making community norms
plain to us.
In this, pastoral letters,
papal encyclicals,
and other such ways of teaching
can help.
Homilies at Masses,
adult education programs in parishes,
forums on issues of our day

all contribute to our understanding
of "the rules"
and how they can support
        our life of faith.

At its worst,
        the church is reduced
        to noisy shouting
                about the law
                and demands that we obey it
                without any further discussion.


At its best,
        the church makes Scripture
        alive for us
                in our everyday life.
It takes the Gospel stories
        and re-tells them
        in such a way
                that our own stories
                begin to merge therein
                and we have the Word of God
                        alive in our hearts
                        and lives.

At its worst,
        the church is reduced
        to mediocre and poor preaching.


At its best,
        the church provides us a way
        and a place to reflect
                on choices in our lives,
                whether major or minor.
It helps us to trust ourselves,
        our intutions and consciences
        and to grow in our ability
                to follow that inner direction,
                knowing it has been formed
                        in the community
                        and will always lead
                        to greater
                and more profound community life.

At its worst,
        the church denies

the value of human experience
　　and mistrusts any intuitions
　　that do not match the rules exactly,
even when those rules
have been arbitrarily established
and are subject to change and development.

At its best,
　　the church provides us a place
　　to find companions
　　　for our journey.
It's a place where kindred spirits
　　can meet
　　and play together.
At its best,
　　the church is a home
　　and being at Mass together every weekend
　　　can draw us in.
At its worst,
　　the church serves as
　　a mere sacramental machine,
　　a place where people come each week,
　　　standing next to each other
　　　without so much as shaking hands
　　　before beginning,
　　and leaving untouched
　　by the profundity of eucharist,
　　by the intimacy of sharing
　　　the bread of life.
At its worst
　　the church is not a place
　　where we break bread together
　　　as companions
　　　but where we break bread alone.
In this case,
　　we impose eucharist
　　on a reality that isn't there,
　　pretending there is community
　　　when there is little or none.

Let's return briefly
　　to the way we began
　　this sequence:

Our conscience, I said,
>   is our deepest inner sanctuary
>   where we find our truest selves.

It's that place
>   where God reveals
>>      our destiny and purpose,
>>      our most private self,
>>      our divine legacy.

It's the place
>   where Sacred Scripture
>>      and Church Teachings
>>      meet our own Human Experience
>>>          to dialogue
>>>          debate
>>>          and decide.

# Listening to God
# in the Prayer
# of Discernment

Prayer is often called a "dialogue"
     between God and us.
But in prayer,
     while we usually speak words toward God,
     whether oral or silent,
          God does not,
          ordinarily,
          speak words back to us.
We don't normally
     hear voices in the tabernacle,
     visions in the night,
     or the skies opening
          and God speaking.
We often pray for things:
     a personal favor,
     a spiritual gift
     a direction in life,
     forgiveness and reconciliation,
     praise and honor of Godself,
     vocational clarity,
     moral direction,
          or whatever....
But do we simply end our prayer
     with our words,
     or does God respond to us somehow?
*In what way does God*
     *ordinarily speak to a person in prayer?*

Karl Rahner wrote of this in
     *Christian at the Crossroads*
     and the Second Vatican Council
          picked up his insights

in its work on prayer and liturgy.
Brian McDermott has written about this
        in his excellent
        *What Are They Saying*
                *About the Grace of Christ?*


God, we would say,
        "speaks" not many words to us,
        but rather *a single word*.
                The word divinely spoken
                is nothing less
                than the life of the one who prays.
For we are aware that God is with us,
        continually creating us,
        constantly loving us,
        and revealing us to ourselves
                and to one another
                at all times.
We are the ones who are spoken in prayer
        and to enter into our lives
        as divine in their source
                and divine in their destiny
                is to enter into prayer.
We are bound up with God
        in such a dramatic way
        that the intricacies of our lives
        are filled with divine energy.
So hearing God
        is hearing our lives
        as they are drawn into God
                in the everydayness
                with which we live.
We aren't waiting for voices from heaven,
        or signs in the night.
No, the voice of God
        is speaking right now in our lives
        when we listen to them as "enlightened"
                by the One who is Light of the World.


We hear God
        speaking within us
        and among us:
                in the inner voices

which make us sure and insistent.
We hear God in the intuitions,
        imaginings,
        and ideas
                which seem to come from nowhere.
We find the Word of God present
        and spoken,
        in our inner voices of conscience,
                in our inner sense of right,
                in our inner place of silence.


But we aren't accustomed
        to listening
        so we often don't hear
                when God speaks like this.
And sometimes we are blocked
        in our hearing
        by psychological,
                ideological,
                sociological,
                or other factors of life.
Any time we try to see ourselves
        apart from God's revelation,
                inspiration,
                or instigation,
        we are mired in a narrow sense of self
        and we are not listening in prayer.
And any time we fail to speak our truths,
        whatever they might be,
        we are blocked in our ability
        to be in touch with the Sacred Energy.
If we withhold or suppress
        areas of darkness,
        memories or dreams,
        hurts, sins, or failures,
        desires, urges, or feelings,
                we stop short
                of full Divine Life.


How can we learn to hear?
        How can we learn to offer
        our full selves in prayer?
Some will require therapy,

others in-depth spiritual direction
but for most people,
    a simple pattern of quiet listening
    will make them prayerful.
Everyone who prays has his or her own method
but these steps seem important
to most people:


First, become comfortable and quiet,
whether sitting
    walking
    driving
    or whatever....
This sort of prayer isn't something
that will necessarily occur
in a chapel
    or at formal prayer.
The sense of the Spirit
with which we are blessed in this
Prayer of Listening
    isn't very easily scheduled.


Second, pause deeply
and allow yourself to relax and rest:
    dropping the shoulders and jaw,
    settling your mind,
    breathing profoundly.
The idea isn't that we must learn
some complex system of exercises
that will guarantee success here.
It's rather that each one of us
learns to relax as we are able.
This relaxing is more
like putting a car in "idle"
than like shifting gears to "park."


Third, bring to mind
that for which you wish to pray:
    a friend soon to visit,
    someone you have wronged,
    a challenging moment,
    a want or need,
    a night dream or a daydream,

your own sense of well-being,
a problem to solve,
a new insight,
or whatever.
You won't have to work very hard at this
because what we have to pray for
is already there,
waiting in our deep minds
to be awakened by this simple way
of paying attention to it.
Bring to mind gently whatever is there,
let it come slowly,
willingly,
and let it linger in the shadows
of your consciousness,
almost at the back of your mind.
If someone were to ask you,
"What's on your mind these days?"
that would be your "agenda" for prayer.
You may wish to mix this "agenda"
with Scripture
spiritual reading
or a reflection on the mysteries
of our faith.


Fourth, watch and listen
to the scene you see and hear.
Pay attention to your own feelings,
ideas,
and imagination.
Be present to the Divine Lover,
the Sacred One.
If you sense resistance,
check that,
for in it you will find
what blocks you.
If you sense light,
follow it gladly.
If you sense darkness,
a hollow feeling,
chaos and great void,
you may be near sinfulness.
If you sense consolation,

that deep sense
of rightness and well-being,
        you are very close to the heart
        of the Lord.

Fifth,
        after a while,
        begin to take in what you hear and see:
        begin to consolidate your thinking,
        begin to mentally record your experience.
Try putting words on it,
        letting it gel,
        and even writing it down a little,
                at least some notes about it.
You may want to share what you have heard
        with others from time to time
        and especially when discerning or praying
                about extremely significant
                or terribly difficult matters.

Sixth, become grateful
        for the gifts you have received
        and know them to have God as Source.
Bask in gratitude for a moment,
        not coming away from your prayer
        until you are ready.
Let your heart swell
        with praise,
        the kind of wordless, speechless awe
                you feel in the face of beauty,
                        love,
                        and generosity.
For you have just seen beauty,
        love,
        and divine, endless generosity.

By this method of letting
        the Divine One
        enter into the "stuff" of our ordinary lives,
                we are drawn into God more and more.
We will feel God's acceptance,
        God's unconditional forgiveness,
        God's urgent call to us

to live as we are created to.
And in this,
        we will be converted
        into ever deeper relationship with God,
        and this will lead us
                to lives of service,
                honesty,
                love,
                and witness.
The everyday details of our lives
        are touched by Divine Presence
        and we come to know deeply
                how to live
                and what choices to make.
If we are faithful to this,
        our consciences will be clear
        and our lifestyles will evidence that.

Part Two

# Contraceptive Birth Control

## Reflection

# How the Church
# Reached a Position
# on Contraception,
# How This Fits into Discernment

During the Second Vatican Council,
        when so many other aspects of Catholic life
        were examined and updated,
        the question of birth control
                was a hot topic.
Before this time,
        the theme of papal teaching
        on birth control
                had been to agree with predecessors.
By and large,
        that meant a re-affirmation of "natural law"
        which required
                that no contraception be used.
But because of the spirit of the times
        and the great amount of discussion
        at Vatican II,
        Paul VI convened a group of people
        known to have excellent credentials
                to advise him about birth control.
He promised a thorough review of the question
        but reserved to himself
        the right to rule in the end.
The commission he convened studied the question
        between 1964 and 1968
        and the pope's decisions were announced
                in July 1968, in a letter
                called *Humanae Vitae.*

At the time,

it seemed to many observers
that church teachers
might be opening the question
of discernment about birth control
to human experience.
It seemed church teachers might be ready to trust
psychology
medicine
sociology
and anthropology a little more.
These modern sciences have informed us
about the human person
in ways unknown to our parents.
In the past 100 years
whole fields of human study have developed
that deepened our understanding
of our minds and hearts,
of our bodies and ourselves.
A virtual revolution in understanding
has occurred
similar to the industrial revolution
which preceded it.
No doubt we still do not understand
all about ourselves
but our recent progress
has been marvelous.


In most human matters,
such as science,
astronomy
medicine
education
politics
economics
and others,
beliefs founded in medieval Europe
before this psychological revolution
are seen as badly out of date
and no longer at the service
of the human family.
Change occurred swiftly in most of these fields
in order to remain current,
in order to remain viable.

Rapid travel developed quickly,
      global communications became available
          almost overnight,
      medicine and psychology kept pace
          with science
          and new "marvels" were announced often.
Science and industry either kept pace
      or were put out of business
      by competitors who did.
We visited the moon,
      added computers to everything,
      and embraced a warmer
          global
          political environment
            eagerly.
Change occurred so rapidly
      it's been difficult to keep pace,
      to keep current maps,
      to even know the names of nations,
          leaders,
          and innovations.


But the church has been slower to change
          than most other fields of endeavor,
          slower to accept human progress
          and development.
A sort of "castle mentality" set in on us
      during the Council of Trent
      in the sixteenth century.
There had been many calls for reform
      in the church
      during the Protestant Reformation.
Luther and his companions wanted
      the kind of reform
      eventually enacted at Vatican II.
Most Catholics would be surprised
      how fully they could give assent
      to the Augsburg Confessions.
But that's today's attitude,
      a new one for Catholics
      and their official teachers in Rome.
In the sixteenth century
      the attitude was one of resistance

because the church saw all this
    call for reform
    as a great danger and threat.
The church saw itself
    a fortress of truth,
    unchangeable, absolute truth,
        which nothing would moderate
        and certainly nothing would change.
At the Council of Trent
    the Roman Church cast itself into concrete
    to prevent change in that century
    and, they hoped,
        in any century to come.
Any who produced evidence
    contrary to church teaching,
    such as Galileo,
        were excommunicated
        or placed under church house arrest.
New ideas were not welcome
    and were seen as a danger to our "castle,"
        something to be avoided
        denied,
        and buried.
This is still pretty much the case today
    in some official circles.
We still silence and "arrest" theologians,
    social thinkers,
    and others.


Nonetheless, Catholic teaching is beginning
    to develop with the times
    even though the official teachers
        often remain resistant
        and the pace is terribly slow.
We have begun to trust
    the work of psychologists
        sociologists
        and anthropologists.
We have begun to see that change
    is necessary
    and even good for the church.
And when it's the moral teachings

of the church that are in question,
it's more necessary than ever
for us to take another look at all this
because the everyday lives and loves
    of so many people
    are directly affected.
We need to ask how the Gospel
    can become more real
    in people's lives today.
We ask how we can refrain
    from imposing seventeeth-century solutions
    on modern challenges and problems.
It's necessary to revisit
    social,
    financial,
    marital,
    relational,
    economic,
    and polictical moral teaching
        because the times demand it.
This is not to say
    that teachings of medieval Europe
    were not perhaps the best they could be
        for that time
        in history.
This is not to say
    that church teaching was once "wrong"
    and is now more "right."
Church teaching always has the responsibility
    to be current,
    to assist the men and women
    of the current time
        to live as fully
        in the ethic of Jesus
        as possible.
Church teaching should always be linked
    to the reality
    of life.
It isn't one-sided but two-sided.
    It is always the church and us!
    It is never just the church
        because we are the church,
        the people of God,

and our official teachers
cannot teach
what no one believes.

So in appointing the commission
on birth control
the pope was moving
in the direction of history,
just as the whole of Vatican II
had itself done.
The pope was asking yet another crucial question,
just as he had about Catholic liturgy
or social justice
or the nature of the church itself
or the role of lay people
or divine revelation
or the transformation of the world.
With the birth control commission,
it seemed our churchly mistrust
of life in the modern world
might be transformed
into partnership with the times
and progress in human generation.

And what did this important commission
recommend to the pope?

A large majority of the commission members
recommended a change
in the church's position
on contraceptive birth control.
As a whole,
the commission urged the pope
to open the possibility
that birth control can sometimes
be a moral good,
and maybe often.
But the commission
also contained a minority
concerned about changing church teaching
on birth control—
or about changing anything!
"If we change this,"

their thinking ran,
"then how can anything else we teach
be believed?
If we change this,
even though there did seem to be a
compelling case to do so,
won't people think other matters may also
be subject to change?
And wouldn't that undermine
the power
and authority
and tradition
of the pope?"
This minority group also had something
to say about sex itself.
Reading what they had to say
is difficult because it's shrouded
in churchy language
which is not the kind
we normally speak to each other
when we're making love!
To sum up their view
we could say they opposed contraception
because sex, in their view,
is for procreation alone
and contraception changes that.
Contraception can have the effect
of making sexual loving
a mutual benefit for the couple
involved.
Such mutual benefit and pleasure
was seen, by this minority,
outside the purposes of sex.
In other words,
their concern was that we would undermine
the purpose of sex
and the dignity of being human
if we allow the mutual benefit
of sexual partners any prominence.

Now, mind you,
this minority was four members
from a commission of about sixty.

But they reported their misgivings
    as a minority report to the pope.
       They urged no change.


The great majority of the commission members,
    however,
    having weighed everything, too,
    reported that some form of contraception
       should be allowed
       or maybe even encouraged.
This majority was less concerned
    with consistency over the centuries
    in papal or church teaching
       and more concerned with the progress
       which the human family has made
       in understanding reproduction
          as a part of life:
          including its psychology and sociology.
This majority report was ready
    to offer Catholics
    a way to make sound Christian choices
    about love and sex and reproduction
    that would make it possible for us
       to live faithfully
       in these modern times.
The majority report
    was concerned that birth control
    not be used "willy-nilly,"
       without helpful reflection
       and discernment.
They were concerned
    that, if chosen by a couple,
    whatever means of birth control is used
       be supportive of human dignity
       and that it be loving,
          that it not undermine
          the beauty of sex.
They were concerned
    that, if chosen,
    it be effective beyond much doubt
    so the purpose of using it
       is not undermined
       by a pre-occupation or fear

of actually becoming pregnant.
They were concerned
        that, if chosen,
        birth control would pose no threat
        to the health of the persons
                or to the welfare
                of our bodies.
And they were concerned
        that the choice
        about how to regulate pregnancy
        be one based on the real life situations
                of the people involved.
To condemn a couple
        to a life of abstinence
        for long periods of time
        as a means of preventing pregnancy
                "cannot be founded on the truth,"
                this majority opinion reported.


But the majority did not prevail
        and the pope ruled with the minority.
                His decision was based
                on their concerns
                about changing long-standing
                church opposition to birth control.
I'm sure he believed
        that in ruling this way
        he was better representing
                the Holy Spirit,
                better articulating
                what God wants for the church.
But his decision has left today's Catholics
        at least in the developed world,
        with difficult choices.
It seems from all pastoral research done today
        that many Catholics find their conscience
        disagrees with this teaching.
We cannot simply write off that disagreement
        by arguing that modern Catholics
        are sex-crazed and selfish.
Many times the choice to prevent conception
        is sound,
                healthy,

and holy.
Sometimes it is also selfish and sinful;
        sometimes it is not generous,
                not truly a well-discerned
                expression of the mutual love
                        of the couple.

Whatever a couple chooses to do,
        the bottom line is not
        birth control itself.
The center-point of the Gospel
        must also be the center-point
        of a decision like this: Love.
Contraception is sinful for a Christian,
        not in and of itself,
        but when it is done by someone
                unwilling to be selfless,
                someone shirking responsibility.
It is sinful, as Dick Westley says,
        when it is entered into out of
                indifference,
                selfishness,
                and any motive that prevents us
                        from being real imitators
                        of Christ.

So the answers to this sensitive question
        are not cut and dried,
        not easy to come to,
        and certainly not reduced
                to the keeping of a law.
It is up to each Catholic couple
        or anyone concerned about
        living in a right relationship
                to weigh church teaching
                alongside other factors
                in the formation of conscience.
It is up to each couple
        to come to terms
        with their own sexual lives
        and to listen closely
        to their own inner sense
                of right.

# Discernment About
# Birth Control

In choosing to regulate
> when you become pregnant,
> and when you don't,
>> the quality of love suggests
>> the decision
>>> should be a shared one.

This concern is a key part
> of church teaching.

If the responsibility
> for getting pregnant or avoiding it
> rests on only the woman
>> or only the man,
>> then an important aspect
>> of shared sexual loving
>>> is compromised.

Sex is,
> by its nature,
>> shared.

Anonymous sex
> or sex where one party
> is unequal to the other
>> doesn't fulfill very well
>> our deep human longing for intimacy
>>> which is really
>>> the basis of sex.

So sex is shared.

The outcomes of sex
> are shared as well.

If the outcome
> is the mutual love of the couple,
> then it seems obvious
>> that cannot be had alone.

If it is mutual,
    it is shared.
Or the outcome may be
    the conception of new life,
    and, even though it is the woman
    whose womb is the temporary home
        of this child,
        still, it is a shared event
        in the life of the couple.

So the decision
    about how to regulate
    when to become pregnant
        is also a shared decision.
And when deciding how to approach
    birth control
    some way of sharing responsibility
        will give the choice
        a firm footing
        in your loving relationship.
No one will feel a "burden"
    is unfairly theirs.

A decision to use a contraceptive,
    a condom,
    abstinence,
    natural family planning or rhythm,
    an intrauterine device,
    or any other means of birth control
        is an important decision
        in our life.
It isn't enough to choose one of these
    simply and carelessly
    without being in touch
        with our deeper selves
        because our sexuality
        is rooted in us
            in very deep,
            very profound ways.
We are deeply
    and profoundly sexual!
Our genitals
    are at the very center

of our bodies
and our primary loving relationships
          at the very center
          of our lives.
We organize how we live
          around who we love
          or don't love.
We are only beginning to understand
          the depth
          and beauty of sex.


In the past
          we have considered sex "dirty"
                    or "sinful."
We considered it
          a "necessary human evil,"
          only appropriate when intending to procreate,
                    as though its mystery and pleasure
                              were from the devil
                              rather than from God.
Our childhoods were, for the most part,
          filled with mixed messages
          about sex.
On one hand
          we were taught it is good and of God,
          the pinnacle of creation.
But on the other,
          we were ordered to silence about it
          and even the simplest questions
                    were shushed and ignored.
We officially taught, on one hand,
          that "natural law"
          is the norm.
But on the other hand,
          we considered the most innocent
          and natural sexual arousal a sin
                    and we called them
                    impure thoughts.
How can a generation of Catholics
          who grew up confessing every sexual urge
          as a "near occasion of sin"
                    not have gotten the message
                    that sex is not good,

that it is, in fact, evil?
This is changing today
    thanks to the ground-breaking work
    of folks like
        John Heagle and Fran Ferder
        Jim Nelson
        Dick Westley
        Matthew Fox
           and others.
We are beginning to provide sex
    a much more sacred place
    in our lives.
Soon, I hope,
    we can also provide it that place
    within the official church.


Who we are
    is intimately and profoundly expressed
    by how we are sexual with others.
Sex is a language
    with which we express
    otherwise inexpressible feelings
        and ancient, eternal truths.
Not only is it
    the way life is transmitted
    and continued on earth,
        it is also
        the most connecting way
        we approach one another.
It's a gift in our lives,
    placed there by the very act
        of conception itself:
           our lives begin with sex
           and we continue life with sex....


So choices about how we will live
    as sexual persons
    are very important to us.
They generate great energy for us
    and great concern.
And they can form a central part
    of our prayer lives
        if we let them.

But how many of us pray about sex?
      How many of us pray
          about birth control?
My suspicion is that
      if we understand prayer
      to be a time of paying attention
          to our deepest inner voices,
          to God's presence in the most creative
          and created parts of ourselves,
             then we pray about this
             more than we think.
We just don't call it prayer.


But decisions about birth control
      will not be made well
      if they're made
      without this deeper look
          into our lives,
          the deeper look which prayer
             can provide.
Therefore, we can approach these choices
      with discernment
      to make them fit us better,
      to be sure that what we do in the end
          is really "right" for us
          is really what our conscience dictates.
Discernment allows us
      to take into account
      the logical and financial aspects
          of choosing
          or not choosing
             to become pregnant
      but it also opens the door
          to more.
Discernment is a process
      of coming to understand and articulate
      as well as we can
          the Divine Mystery within us,
          the Word present in our core,
          the deepest part of our being.
It is a process that is on-going
      and puts us in touch
      with our "real" selves

in ways that logic or law alone
can fail to do.
When we've discerned well,
we come away with a deep feeling
of consolation.
We come away knowing
in our bones,
in our gut,
that we are doing what is right.
Our "real" selves
are not always logical—
as anyone in love knows already.
Our moods and feelings,
our intuitions and imaginings,
our dreams and hopes
do not always fit logically
into slots
like pegs into same-shaped holes.
We are all artists
when it comes
to this part of our lives,
all subject to impulses,
desires,
and attractions
which we do not intend
and cannot easily anticipate.

So, unlike the process
of reaching logical decisions,
or simply, blindly following a law,
discernment about birth control
will allow us
to take this into account.
It will allow us
to be in touch
with God speaking to us
in those deep parts of us
where common language
is no longer sufficient,
those parts where we can only sense
what we feel
and can often not find words,
spoken words,

to describe our inner selves.
Discernment can assure us
that the choice
we are making
will be rooted
in the Divine Mystery,
the Force of Life
and Love.

# In Gratitude for Sex

We greet you,
>O God of Creation,
>you who are Mother and Father
>>to us all.

We greet you as the people we are,
>perfect yet imperfect,
>healthy yet unhealthy
>whole yet incomplete.

And we thank you
>for the most wonderful part of us,
>that part which is so full of pleasure
>>yet can lead to so much pain:
>>>our sex.

We thank you for filling us
>with urges
>and desires
>and attractions
>>for one another.

We thank you for putting within our very soul
>the drive to unite in sex:
>>profoundly,
>>entirely,
>>and pleasurably;
>>>a foretaste of our unity with you.

We thank you for our hearts
>and our bodies,
>for our tastes and smells
>for the pleasures of our eyes
>>as we gaze upon our beloved
>>as we watch them unnoticed
>>as we see them returning to us
>>>when they've been absent.

We thank you for the wonderful feel
>of touch,
>the great pleasure of being held

and stroked
and rubbed.

But above all,
we thank you for the inexpressible joy,
that fully, uniquely human ecstacy
of being chosen and wanted,
of being made to feel important,
of being found beautiful
by another:
by our beloved.
And of being able to express that
in the language of sex:
that most profound way
of speaking love.
O God,
we dance with this joy,
we exult in it.
Like the dolphins dancing in the sea
or the deer playing in the forest,
or the laughter of innocent children,
so do our hearts leap up
and so do our souls fill.
The wonderful unity of body and spirit
which is our lives
can only have come
from your own powerful oneness.
And the even more wonderful unity
which our love and our sex
produces between and among us
can only be a sign of you.
Central to our bodies
and central to our lives,
as the pinnacle of your creative burst,
we thank you for making us capable
of this:
to celebrate sex
to take pleasure in orgasm
and to participate
in your creative work.
And when that creative work
leads to the conception of a new life,
your wonder

is even more fully expressed!
Living and wondrous signs,
    permanent witnesses to the moment
    where two people embrace in love,
        conceived in sex
        and borne with hope;
            born with pain
            and nurtured for life: our child.
We do not know the exact moment
        of conception;
        this is a moment known only to you.
But we do know
        at that great moment
        the entire code of life is present
            as the first cells
            of the new person are joined
            in secret.
We know your powerful hand
        is present
        and we know that here again,
            in this new man or woman,
            you will be present.

O God,
        Creator
        Sustainer
        Force of Life
        Source of Truth,
            turn our hearts in gratitude today
            for sex
            and for its outcomes:
                life and love.
For our bodies,
        perfect or imperfect:
            our lips and eyes
            our arms and chests
            our stomachs and hips
            our genitals
            our thighs and legs
            our feet and toes
            our musk and scents.
For our sexual attractions
        which lead us to each other
        in ways so profound

we can only symbolize their meaning
but never speak it entirely.
For the mystery of love
the unspeakable generosity we have
toward each other.
And above all,
O God,
we are grateful for this gift:
the graceful, awkward moment
of sex and love,
the silent, noisy moment,
the ugly, beautiful moment,
the moment of sex and love
which is both alluring
yet somehow frightening.
We turn in gratitude today
because we know in our bones
in our eternal, shared souls,
that this moment
is our most profound moment with you.

## LifeSong

# I'm Afraid
# I Might Be Pregnant!

O God,
>  I think I might be pregnant
>  but I hope to hell
>  >  I'm not!

We wanted to be so careful
>  not to let this happen again.

We wanted to enjoy
>  our love
>  but also have no more children.

Is there something so wrong in that?

I love,
>  dearly love,
>  the children we have, O God.

Each of them is a gift
>  and each of them has led John and me
>  >  closer to you.

Brian with his keen eye for life
>  and his bright mind
>  has exposed us to thoughts
>  >  and insights we would never have known.

MaryAnn is a miniature of me,
>  filling the kitchen and house
>  and all of our stomachs
>  >  with food
>  >  and laughter
>  >  and sometimes,
>  >  >  quiet, tearful moods.

And Lenny,
>  forts and fishing and farting
>  mixed with Beethoven and Bach
>  >  and brilliance!

And Maura!
>  Little Maura!

51

I'm afraid we might have spoiled her
            a little
            but the other kids
            wouldn't let us.
O God,
        these kids are wonderful gifts
        and they fill our lives
                with constant joy
                and also pain
        but we, I, am grateful, nonetheless.


But it's been seven years,
        nearly eight,
        and it isn't "time" any more for me.
I realize my body can still bear children
        but the right time for us
        for me,
                is passed now.
It's my time for other work,
        my LifeWork
        and I've just re-started that
                and it feels so right to me
                to be back.


*Pause*


I know,
        Good God of All,
        that you do not make people pregnant.
I know that you are not intervening
        in my life
        in this way today.
I know that,
        if I'm indeed pregnant,
        it's because John and I didn't do all we could
                to prevent this.
But...
        ...the church still says...
        And I know
                that's no excuse either
                because we both have a conscience
                and we can both make adult decisions
                and we are both responsible.

So here I stand
>at the kitchen sink
>alone this morning,
>>crying into my coffee,
>>and I'm not even sure yet
>>that I am really pregnant.
I mean,
>I'm 45 years old, after all,
>and I might simply be missing
>>my period.
>It's about that time for me.
I hope that's what this is about
>because I don't know how I would handle
>>having
>>and raising
>>and loving another child right now.
I don't want another child. Period.

*Pause*

But,
>if I am actually pregnant
>we will love number five with all our hearts
>and we will work together
>>as a family
>>to be sure this baby
>>knows and understands unconditional love.
We will borrow a crib
>and newborn clothing
>and toys
>and we will make this baby at home here
>>and give it no cause
>>to ever doubt its place among us.
We will find the time
>and the energy
>and the devotion for this baby
>and we will go forward
>>without ever looking back.

But that doesn't change the fact
>that I think I might be pregnant
>and I hope to hell
>>I'm not.

# LifeSong

## A Couple's Secret Thoughts
## About a Vasectomy

— Doug —

I love her so much.
　　　　I never dreamed I would live
　　　　with someone like her,
　　　　　　　　never thought I'd be the lucky one
　　　　　　　　to love and be loved by so wonderful
　　　　　　　　a woman.
She brings life to our house,
　　　　her voice lilting in the morning,
　　　　　　　deep in the night,
　　　　　　　filled with laughter or tears
　　　　　　　　　steady,
　　　　　　　　　strong,
　　　　　　　　　confident,
　　　　　　　　　　　and here....
Our days together,
　　　　even when the kids are around,
　　　　are filled with tender,
　　　　　　　gently affectionate,
　　　　　　　reassuring moments.
In a sense,
　　　　I guess,
　　　　you could say we live our love
　　　　　　　every day.
We love each other so much.

— Nancy —

I can't imagine loving anyone more
　　　　than I do Doug.
I love him most
　　　　when he's just around the house,

hovering near me.
When I look up from my desk
      and see him there,
      standing at the sink,
      one kid at his left leg
            and another at his right,
            I can scarcely hold myself back.
I want to run to him
      throw my arms around him
      and make love to him right there.
We've been married,
      by the way,
      for 17 years.
So this isn't some new, puppy-love
      sort of thing in me,
      but a permanent, profound love.
Oh, we've had our tough times:
      fights,
      silence,
      distance,
      fears.
We went through a period two years ago
      when things seemed pretty rocky
            and unsure.
I was pregnant,
      unplanned, mind you,
      and this was number four for us.
My moods were unpredictable,
      even to me,
      and some days I couldn't stand him,
            period.
There was nothing he could say or do
      and really,
      nothing I could either.
But before Michael was born
      something happened,
      something mysterious that we still
            haven't really figured out,
            and our devotion to each other
            has been strong ever since.
The birth was difficult,
      my first C-section,
      and we were both afraid

but Michael was beautiful after all
and we do love him.


— Doug —

I was so worried for her,
        for her health.
And I guess I felt a little selfish,
        too; I wanted her
        and didn't want to share her
                with any more children.
Is that so bad?
        Is it so wrong to come to a point
        where you draw the line
                and start asking for time
                for yourself?
Anyway, I wasn't exactly a model husband
        during her last pregnancy.
I'm not sure what happened
        between us.
I just felt distant
        and silent
        and angry, I think.
I felt angry that she was pregnant
        but I don't think I realized that
        until now.
I mean,
        it wasn't exactly her fault,
        after all,
        and we do love Michael.
But Nancy had just gone back to teaching
        before this happened
        and I knew how important that was to her.
And let's face it,
        how much more stress could there be
        on the human body
                than being pregnant?
She's 37, almost 38,
        and I know it took her much longer
        to recover from Michael
                than from the others.
It isn't that she's unhealthy,

mind you,
just that she's getting,
well, toward middle age.
One of my friends at the gym
asked whether we'd ever heard
of birth control.
He seemed to suggest maybe we didn't want
Michael.
But that isn't true.
We love him. We didn't plan on him
but we do love him.

— Nancy —

We've decided not to get pregnant again.
We, I, don't want another baby.
But so far,
our plan hasn't worked so well.
We haven't had sex for three months now
because my period is still a little
unpredictable.
I don't want to start now
with some sort of contraceptive
because I don't know what might happen
to me.
I hate to mess around with my body
right now.
I just had a baby nine months ago
and I'm still not back to normal
and I don't want to do something that would
hurt me.
Doug doesn't want me to either.
So we aren't having sex right now
and it's killing us.

— Doug —

Last night we had a fight,
our first in months.
We haven't had sex for...
God! it must be almost half a year now!
It feels like forever.

To me, at least.
So here we are:
in our late thirties,
four kids,
two careers,
a busy home,
and no sex.
We're in the time of our life
when we most need each other
as we sort out how to respond
to our fifteen year old
and our twelve year old
and our eight year old
not to mention Michael.
We need pillow talk,
we need one another
lovingly, warmly, definitely!
But we can't have sex right now
because we really can't risk
another pregnancy.
Abortion would be out of the question
for us,
absolutely out.
Birth control?
I don't want her using any chemicals
in her body
because this is such
a sensitive time in her life.
I'm seriously thinking
about a vasectomy.

— Nancy —

I know the church says having a vasectomy
is wrong
but I wish Doug would have one.
They're against them
because they say it makes a person
"unnatural."
It takes away fertility,
and makes a person "less human"
or something.
But nothing could be less natural

than how we're living right now;
nothing could be less human
than living without sex for us,
without our evenings together in bed.
It isn't just the sex we miss;
we don't even have foreplay any more
because we know we can't risk
a foolish mistake.
He used to come up behind me sometimes
in the evening
and put his arms around me
and kiss my neck and blow into my ear
and whisper to me.
I used to take baths in candlelight and cologne
and wear that nightie he gave me
for our anniversary.
He used to sit with the kids
doing their homework,
winking at me and grinning
about what we'd do later.
And I used to love it!

I want him so much
and I know he wants me
but we are apart now.
I think the church wants us to live
"as sister and brother,"
waiting until I am through menopause,
until we can have sex again
without getting pregnant.
I'll tell you something about that
kind of thinking:
it's nuts.
I need him now.
I want his strong arms,
his gorgeous chest,
his legs pressing against mine.
I want him. Period.
And I can't wait ten years
until I'm through menopause.
That could destroy our wonderful marriage,
hurt the kids,
bring darkness into our home.

The glow of love
        is what we need now,
                not darkness.

The one thing I worry about
        is his self-image
        if he does this.
Will he feel like less of a man
        if he has a vasectomy?


                —Doug —


I wonder if Nancy
        will still find me masculine
        if I have this done.
I mean,
        it isn't like anything will change,
        on the outside,
        and I can't imagine losing any desire
                for her
                by doing this.
I know, too,
        that this is wrong
        at least in the eyes of the church
        but I wonder when one of them
                was in my position.
I wonder when one of them
        faced this impossible choice:
        no sex or possible pregnancy.
Even if Nancy died next year
        I wouldn't want to father another child.
Good grief,
        I'd have my hands full
        with just these four.
Even if I re-married,
        I can't imagine myself
        wanting to father any more children.
It wouldn't even be responsible
        to think of it.


                — Nancy —


We'll talk tonight, I know,

and I hope we decide something.
I miss him terribly
        and want him back to me soon.


                — Doug —


We'll talk tonight.
        I have some apologizing to do
        about what I said last night to her
                and I want her to know
                how sorry I am.
I love her so much
        and I want her back again;
        more now than ever....

Part Three

# Quitting a Commitment

# Why It Is Often Good
# to Celebrate the Outcomes
# of Careful Discernment

Sometimes the right thing to do
    is to get a divorce
    or leave religious life
    or end your active ministry as a priest.
Sometimes the right thing to do
    will surprise you
        with its stark reality,
        with its finality,
        with its harsh public response.
Sometimes it's necessary
    for us
    to make the tough choice
        in order to make the right choice.

And when that happens,
    when we do what we know deep within us
    is most right for us,
        then it's also time
        to celebrate!
We want to celebrate divorce,
    not because it's a happy thing to go through
    or because it's time for a party,
        but to ritualize
        and solemnize it
            when it's a "right discernment."
We want to celebrate a priest's
    "Last Mass"
    just as we do his first,
        when his choice to leave
        is really a choice to move on
            to something that better represents
            his own calling.

We want to celebrate a decision
    to leave religious vows
    when the person making that difficult choice
        is responding faithfully
        to an inner call,
        in the sanctuary of conscience.

"Right discernments,"
    whether to begin something
    or to end it,
        deserve celebration.
They are the outcome of prayer
    and divine leadership in our lives,
    the outcome of painful searches for truth
        and earnest attention
        to our true selves.
We celebrate them because
    following a right discernment
    leads to wholeness and holiness.

Beginning and ending
    chapters of our lives
    is filled with both sadness and joy.
Beginning is full of sadness
    because nothing can be begun
    unless something else is ended.
Birth always involves pain,
    struggle,
    a giving up of something
        in order to have or be something else.
It's also full of joy
    because we begin what we believe
    we are called to do.
We begin what we hope will fulfill us,
    help us become what we sense
        we are created to be.
So beginning a marriage
    or religious life
    or the priesthood
        has an element of apprehension
        and dying to self.
And, of course,
    such beginnings also are times of joy.

Leaving such commitments
    creates in us the same sentiments.
It's filled with joy,
    tempered joy,
    when we've discerned it well
        but it's also filled with sadness
        because leaving is really nothing more
        than beginning something new.

Celebrating these moments of life
    with a ritual
    where friends,
        family,
        and colleagues gather
        to witness our well-made decision
    brings together the sadness of leaving
    with the happy certainty of inner peace.
It allows us to share with others
    what we know to be true ourselves:
    that we have made a legitimate choice
        and a valid discernment.

We have often been reluctant
    to celebrate such decisions.
As a church
    and a culture
    we have often heaped shame
    on folks whose life paths
        lead them to change.
We've developed the thinking
    that living in one state in life
    for all our lives,
        no matter what,
        is better than changing
        even when it's perfectly clear
            that change would be more holy.

Here's the conventional thinking
    on this:
    "Good people" stay married
        or in vows
        or in active ministry as priests
            for life.

"Weak,
indecisive,
confused,
irresponsible people"
        change their minds
        and leave.
We tend to punish
        divorcees
        ex-nuns
        ex-seminarians
        and ex-priests
                by labelling them that way
                for life.
You've heard someone say
        of you or of someone else,
        "She's in her second marriage, you know..."
                which is really to say,
                "She's a floosy, you know...
                        can't keep a mate."
Or, "He's an ex-priest.
        They say he can't make up his mind...."


But God stays with us
        when we leave a vow
        even if our family
                or bishop
                or culture
                or friends shut us out.
Many communities of women religious
        celebrate leave-taking this way.
Part of the Jewish community
        celebrates divorce this way.
And ancient peoples had a keen sense
        when it was time for someone to leave,
                whether to move on,
                to marry,
                to divorce,
                or even to die.
They said their good-byes
        and bid their sister or brother well
                for the journey to come.


I think the church

has been reluctant to honor and celebrate
such changes in people's lives
because of its view of vocations
            as absolute and final
                        callings from God.
No doubt, a vocation is divine in its source
            but, as Thomas Merton has put it,
                        a vocation is not the result
                        of a supernatural lottery.
Like all God's creative work,
            vocations unfold gradually.
They don't hit us
            like hard news
            or bricks falling from the sky.
Nonetheless,
            we tend to think that at some point
            when we make the commitment
            to enter into a vow
                        the gradual unfolding stops,
                        the development of our vocation ends.
That just isn't true,
            however,
            and modern psychology is helping us
                        understand that well.

We also tend to think like this:
            God has given us the gift of marriage
                        or the priesthood
                        or religious life,
                        and a gift once given thus
                                    cannot be taken away.
If we have received and accepted the gift
            of our vocation,
            in other words,
                        we can expect to receive
                        no more such gifts.
In other words,
            we tell people
            that God's mind doesn't change
            and ours shouldn't change either.
"God will give us the strength and grace
            to stay with it
            so don't give up."

There are many flaws in this way of thinking
       about vocations,
       chief among them that God's continuing work
          in our lives
          might very well be thwarted
          by our insistence
              that our official position
              on this is right
              and people's consciences are not.
Let us continually listen
       to the voice of God within us
          so that we can continually discern
          how we are called.
The norm certainly may be that we are called
       into a lifework
       which will not change.
But isn't it possible that some people
       may be called on?
Isn't it possible that situations change
       or that there wasn't complete ability
          to give full consent
          at the time of the original vow?
Isn't it possible that our spouse
       or community members
       may have become violent toward us?
Isn't it possible that some folks
       may be called to more than one work?
          more than one task in life?
          more than one place
              or community
              or church
              or family?
Isn't it possible
       that we don't know everything
       about the human heart,
          or maybe not very much at all?

For who can know the mind of God?
       Who can plumb the depths of God's wisdom?
       Who can know what may lie ahead
          for any one of us?
Who can know
       what terrible personal violence may be done

by failing to move on,
by failing to leave that vow?
We must always be mindful
that God's ways,
known in the secret of the heart,
are not our ways.
And we are required
to have great humility
to learn this lesson
and to celebrate with ourselves or others
when we respond to it.
We are called,
if we are called to anything at all,
to fidelity beyond a human promise.
We are not called to faith in an institution
but to faith in the Lord,
in the Force of Life,
in the Source of All.


When someone responds,
says "Yes!" to their calling,
whether to begin or to end a state in life,
we want to celebrate
that as an affirmation
of the divine presence
in our midst.
We want to celebrate
with this sister or brother
to honor and support them
because in doing so
we are expressing faith
in the Mystery which we name:
"God."

# The Choices
# Are Never Easy

Sometimes there's nothing left
    to celebrate
    except that this is the end.
Sometimes the married or vowed life
    becomes violent
        cruel
        or filled with infidelity.
Some are loaded with alcohol and drugs,
        manipulation,
        and coercive sex.
For such marriages,
    their only hope might be in their end.
This is true especially for women
    on whom violence is heaped
        without mercy.

The breakdown in a relationship
    or a promise
    or a marriage
        is no small matter.
One of God's sure signs among us
    is permanence,
        fidelity,
        stability,
        and long suffering.
God is with us always.
    God's love is constant,
    never-ending,
        and eternal.
Our hope is to model that
    in our own lives
    in such a way that we, too,
        are a sign to the world.
Our hope when we marry,
    or commit ourselves to the church

is that we will live in that promise
for life.
So a choice to move on
is not taken lightly
and is a matter for intense discernment
and great care.
In our society we tend
to be a bit casual
regarding these things.
"Oh well,"
we hear folks say sometimes,
"I guess it just didn't work out."

But sometimes what might not be working
is the inner life of the one
who makes the choice to leave.
Sometimes it's a terrible mistake
to leave a marriage
or religious life
or the priesthood.
Sometimes our reasons for moving on
are to escape the demands of the Gospel,
not to embrace them more fully.

This is hard news for modern people
who want what they want
no matter what.
The journey to a commitment made in love
is one walked with the Divine Guide,
one walked with a partner
or spiritual director.
It's a journey of life,
one that takes in all parts of us
and considers every angle
and makes the choice to say "Yes!"
Likewise, the journey to leave such a choice
must be one made slowly,
made with the Divine Guide once again,
made with others
who can guide us.
For some that journey to leave
will begin
and prove to be nothing more

than a passing fancy.
We get bored, after all,
    so easily
    or we see "greener grass"
    or envy others' freedom.
We want self-fulfillment so much sometimes
    that we place ourselves first,
    rather than last:
        but..."the last shall be first."
What does this mean for us?
    What does it mean?


For others, the journey
    will turn up life issues forgotten
        or ignored
        or repressed
            which demand attention
            before another commitment
                is made.
For still others,
    this journey will be one
    that does lead them to new freedom,
        new depths of God's presence,
        and new understandings of vocation.
Those who wish to remarry
    after a divorce or a leaving of vows
    deserve our trust.
There isn't any doubt a decision to remarry
    should be made carefully,
    should be one that takes into full account
        the reasons for the breakdown
        of the first promise.
But must it involve a church court?
    Must it involve canon lawyers
    testimony,
    and hearings?
Might it not be possible for us to approach this
    with more compassion
    than mistrust?
Carl Jung has figured out that change
    can sometimes be a moment of grace
        for us.
For many folks,

divorce,
the leaving of vows,
and other difficult life choices,
        are indeed such moments of grace.
We should be careful
        not to treat them harshly.
Whatever the case in this,
        the choices are always difficult,
        the grief may be deep,
        and the persons walking this journey
                are worthy of compassion
                        understanding,
                        and love.

# A Woman's Lament
# Over a Marriage
# Devoid of Love

Roger,
>how do I begin to tell you
>what's on my mind
>>and in my heart
>>these cold November days?

It's not easy for a woman
>to tell the man she married
>what I want to tell you tonight.

We've been married
>almost 36 years.
>Thirty-six years is a long time.

I look at our wedding pictures
>from time to time
>and I see two young people
>>who scarcely knew each other,
>>who barely knew themselves.

Sometimes, to be honest,
>I wonder why we got married.

There was so much I didn't know
>about you then,
>so many mysteries,
>so many unrevealed secrets,
>>so much to learn about each other.

But after 36 years
>I'm not sure I know you
>any better now
>>than I did then.

When did the season of winter
>enter our marriage?
>When did we go cold on each other?
>When did the blossom
>>of our early love

wilt and fail?
I've been waiting,
        hoping,
        praying
        that spring would come again
                and melt the ice
                which has kept our communication frozen
                for so many years.

When is the last time
        we really talked with each other?
We've done a good job of talking to,
        or at one another,
        but we never really listened,
                did we?

It's hard for me to accept
        that we drifted apart from each other.
The kids made me forget
        the alienation I felt
        in those silent hours
                when I waited hopefully,
                always so hopefully,
                that you would come to bed one night
                        and talk to me,
                                to Me.
The bed,
        *our* bed, Roger,
        was the lonliest place in the house
                for me. It was the place
                        I wanted you most,
                        the place you might have opened up
                                to me,
                                might have been naked.
In the end
        that bed was the coffin of our marriage,
                wasn't it?
        Lifeless, loveless bodies,
                laying, waiting,
                        dying.

You stopped offering me your hand
        to hold on to

when Tommy came along.
Then, one after the other,
    the kids were born
    and, with four children,
        my hands were so full
        that at first I didn't notice
        you were gone.
So we both held on to the hands
    of our children
    forming a fragile chain
    between us.
With each child,
    a new link was added
    but the chain was never enough
    to bind us together,
        to help us reach each other.
A dark chasm was opening between us.

When I noticed
    you were absent more often
    it magnified the
        bitterness
            anger
            and hurt
    I'd already been feeling.
Time after time
    you chose anything or anyone
    other than me
    and I hated you for it.
The pain and resentment I harbored
    grew like wild weeds
    choking the life from our marriage.
I felt neglected
    taken for granted
    and unrespected.
Instead of telling you,
    I fell silent.
    I should have left,
        I wanted to leave you,
        but where would I have gone?

We filled our lives
    with other activities

so we wouldn't have to confront
the reality of our dying marriage.
Then, one by one,
our children left:
Thomas
Sara
Ellen.
As each one moved away,
I heard the quiet grow in our house
and I silently panicked
as the chain between us grew smaller.
Gradually we had to face each other then
but realized,
didn't we?
that there wasn't much left
for us to face.
We'd grown apart for so long
that we were living alone together
and pretending.
I clung to those kids,
oh I clung to them
because I knew when they left,
the energy of our life together
would be gone, too.

Soon Peter will be leaving.
Whose hand
will I hold then?
Whose?

*Pause*

Roger,
I want
a divorce.
There. I've said it out loud.

*Pause*

Why can't I tell you this?
Why can't I say to you
what I can say to myself
as I gaze out the kitchen window

into this dark night?
You're not home tonight
        and I don't know where you are
        but I know I can't see you any more.
Standing here now,
        my hands in this dishwater,
        all I can see is my own sad reflection
                in this window,
                this night mirror,
                        me here alone,
                        a prisoner.

# A Man Wonders
# What Happened
# to His Dreams of Love

Care for a cup of coffee?
    No, I don't suppose you do;
    too late for the caffeine, I'm sure.
Well, I'll have one.
    I don't have to worry about not sleeping,
    I won't sleep anyway.
I haven't really slept for months,
    maybe a year or more.
That situation between Sarah and me:
    it's on my mind night and day.
I just can't seem to understand it:
    can't forget it
    and can't figure it out.

I know I loved her when I married her,
    at least I *think* I did.
We weren't kids. I was almost 25 then.
    She was beautiful to me,
    a real knock-out.
We met at a dance at Country Roads.
    Remember that place?
    I met a lot of girls there.
        That's where Donny met his wife,
        but, of course, they're still in love.
I saw Donny last week
    shopping with his family
    in town.
They looked so happy,
    so, I don't know, "together...."

Anyway, for the first couple years,
    Sarah and I got along great.
We went places together
    and laughed

and we even argued then...
          ...but we always made up.
Then Tony was born,
          and John followed two years later
          and something started to unfold in her,
                    something I hadn't seen before.
I'd come home and she'd be mad,
          accusing me of things,
          even implying maybe I was steppin' out
                    a little.
I fought back, mad myself.
          I must admit, I do have a temper.
          But she deserved it, accusing me like that.
She didn't think I respected her,
          didn't think I gave her much time.
          She wanted me home more...
                    ...but I had work to do.
She had this ideal family in mind
          you know where mom and dad
          and all these happy kids
                    in cute J.C. Penney outfits
                    go driving along the highway
                    in a wood-paneled station wagon....
Sort of like Doris Day and Rock Hudson
          in her mind.
Well, we weren't like that.
          I'm no Rock Hudson
          and she's certainly no Doris Day.

We fought in front of the kids sometimes
          which I know wasn't right
          but how do we know when things
                    are gonna blow up?
It got worse and worse
          and I didn't know what to do.
I just stayed away more
          and the more I did that
          the more she complained
                    and the more she complained
                    the more I hated her....

Then Kandra was born,
          a beautiful little girl

who looks just like Sarah.
For a few months everything settled down
        and I thought maybe we'd just had a phase,
        you know, one of them "passages"
                or whatever.
But one night when Kandra was almost a year old
        I came home
        and there was Sarah
        with one of her girlfriends.
They were sitting in the kitchen
        and they were drunk!
There was some country western station
        playing real loud on the radio
        and they were giggling and laughing
                and when I came in
                her girl friend said,
                "Ooops, here comes trouble!"
I lost it. The fight we had that night
        was the turning point I think.
I embarrassed her in front of her friend
        and I drove her away from me.
        I don't think she's ever been back.
Our bed became a deep freeze;
        it's hard to imagine
        how she got pregnant again.
When Sammy was born,
        I said that was it,
        no more kids.
We had enough troubles
        and I didn't want more kids
        to make things worse.

But things got worse for us,
        worse and worse.
She was drinking and I was gone
        and when we did see each other
        we fought.
I don't think the kids saw a minute of love
        between us,
        no hugs, no kisses, no tenderness,
                nothing at all.
All they saw and all they heard
        was ugly.

I worked day and night,
        mostly to avoid the house
        and her
        and my own life.
I guess I was avoiding myself, really,
        not wanting to face my decisions.
Here I was married to someone
        I didn't think I loved,
        sleeping with her every night,
        raising a bunch of kids,
            wondering how the hell I got into this
            and how the hell I'd ever get out of it.
I was gone but she was, too.
        The kids went to the neighbors
        for love.
That hurt me no end.

She had wild ideas,
        crazy notions about me:
        thinking I was with other women,
        thinking I wanted her dead.
I'd get so mad sometimes
        I'd yell at her
        and say stuff I didn't even mean.
I tried to hurt her
        and the kids saw that
        but they saw how nuts she'd become, too.
They knew she was drinking,
        that she and her damn girl friends
        were wild.
Then she started staying out all night sometimes
        and I didn't know what to do.
I didn't have anyone to talk to, really.
        We don't talk about this kind of stuff
        in my family much.
We just try to pretend
        everything's normal all the time
        even when it's mixed up and goofy.

Two years ago she decided she wanted
        a divorce,
        wanted to move to Maine
            with her girl friend

and leave the kids with me.
I said, "No way to that."
I said no because divorce is wrong
          in my mind.
          It seems too easy, too quick.
"Can't we work this out?" I thought.
Really I was just avoiding the obvious
          and the eventual.
She stayed for a while,
          if you could call what she was doing
          "being here."
She was gone all the time,
          no warning,
          I never knew where she was.
She used to come dragging in
          in the middle of the night
                    sometimes,
          all drunk up, smelling like cigarettes.


Then one night that winter, I came in the house
          and found the kids there alone.
Johnny was crying in his bedroom
          and Tony was mad.
When I got there
          he took me on. He's only 12
          but he knows what's on his mind.
"Get outta here!" he screamed at me.
          "You don't even love us,
          mom don't love us neither.
                    Just leave us alone."
"Tony," I said, moving toward him,
          "listen, honey..."
But he wouldn't have it!
          "Just get out!"
          and he pounded on me with his fists,
          pushing me back toward the door.
"Just get out and leave us alone!"
          But I caught his arms
          and knelt down in front of him
          and his screaming turned into tears.
                    He wailed into my shoulder,
                    crying his heart out.
He was so afraid,

so frightened we would abandon them.
He's the oldest, you know,
>and he was sort of taking over the family
>right then.
I held him tight as he sobbed
>and he held on tight
>really wanting me to stay,
>>not to leave.
I could see over his shoulder
>that Kandra was hiding under the table
>in the dining room
>and little Sammy was peeking around the corner
>>from the kitchen,
>>both of them scared as hell.
I looked around.
>The house was a mess,
>the kids were dirty,
>their mother was gone,
>and I was emotionally absent
>>and for the most part
>>gave them no time either.
They looked like waifs or orphans to me
>that night.
>And then I did something
>>I hadn't done for years.
I started to cry myself.

I made up my mind that night
>things would change around that house.
I realized that I would have to change,
>too. This mess was as much
>>my fault as anyone's.
I was too proud,
>too stubborn,
>too damn afraid of tenderness,
>too threatened as a "man"
>>to ever give an inch.
I crouched there holding my son,
>and considered our options.
Maybe we're just very different people
>and we'll end up with a divorce.
I know the church says that's wrong
>but the guys who wrote those rules

weren't living in this house
        and they haven't heard this kid
        here in my arms
        crying because his parents
                don't love each other.
They think love just comes easy,
        or that its automatic
        or something.
But it isn't and sometimes love leaves you
        and it don't really matter
        whose fault it is when that happens.
Sometimes you just get to a point
        where nothing else can be done.
The guys who wrote those rules
        had a good idea:
        marriage should be forever, I agree.
But they weren't living in this house,
        they weren't struggling
                with love gone cold.
So, I thought that night,
        either I stay with her
        and live with this mess
                or I get divorced
                and live with that
                        the rest of my life.
Either way I lose;
        either I live with pain,
        or I live with guilt and shame.
Oh I know, I can try to get an annulment
        from the church,
        but what's that about?
Are they going to say we never had a marriage
        to start with?
That ain't true.
We did love each other once,
        I know we did.
        We really thought this was for life;
                we really were married.
And I don't know what happened here,
        Who does?
Do some strangers reading a rule book
        think they can figure out
        what makes love go cold like this?

Do they think they can unravel
            the heart of this woman
            and find out what's there?
I know I might need some help,
            maybe someone to talk to
            or even some counselling or something,
                        but I don't need a church court
                        for that!
What I need right now
            is a friend,
            not a judge.

*Pause*

Well, Sarah did finally come home that night
            two winters ago,
            and she had someone with her
                        but it wasn't a girl friend.
They got some of her stuff
            and she said she'd call
            and out they went.
I slept with all the kids
            in our bed that night
            and the next day I cleaned the house
                        and took the kids out of school
                        to go shopping together.
We started over
            and Tony's been my right-hand man.
John and Kandra both got As
            in spelling this week
            and Sammy read his first "real" book
                        to me
                        last night.

She comes to visit every other weekend
            and talks with the kids
            and actually loves them very much.
There's no fighting in the house any more
            and you can tell it on the kids.
They don't hide in their rooms,
            or fight as much
            and they aren't as "jumpy" as they were.
I'm better, too,

less moody,
less absent.

Believe it or not,
    I think she really loves that guy
        she married.
She seems happy.
    Maybe the kids were too much,
    maybe she never loved me at all,
    maybe she just needed a break
        or a change,
        or a new lover.

I started dating someone myself
    last year
    and we were married this month.
Her name is Mary
    and she's beautiful,
        so much backbone,
        such a prayer life.
She really loves these kids
    and she even gets along pretty well
        with Sarah.
Two weeks ago
    they went together to take the kids
    shopping for school clothes.
        Mary could get along with anyone!
I know I'm on very thin ice here
    as far as the church is concerned
    and I'm sure they mean well
        with their rules
        and all.
I realize I'm a little over the edge
    of what they permit
    for people like me,
        sexually, I mean.
And I realize I can't really go to communion
    any more either.
I don't think what Mary and I are doing
    is such a great sin
    but I know the church says it is.
I don't see how they can claim
    that this kind of love,

even if it's a little imperfect,
            is a sin.
But I do realize it's against the rules
            and I'm trapped
            so I take the kids to Mass
            and when they get up to go to communion
                        I just stand and let them pass
                                    in front of me.

It's funny,
            for the first time
            in a dozen years,
            almost since we were married,
                        I feel love and tenderness
                        with someone.
I finally feel accepted and affirmed,
            vulnerable,
            open,
            and honest.
All the darkness of those years
            with Sarah,
                        the fights and mistrust,
                        the hate and violence,
                                    is finally gone.
Our home is a place of light
            and love
            and prayer...
...and now I'm unable to receive communion.
It's funny,
            sort of.

# On Leaving
# Religious Life

Where, O Spirit of God,
        are you leading me?
I laugh at the unpredictability
        of your call.
I really do not know
        where you're leading me
        at this time in my life.
I can't see what's coming
        and I can barely get a grasp
            on what's passed by for me
            these past weeks.

In these recent months
        your prompting deep within
        has urged me to prepare
            for a new journey.
Like a sudden gust of wind,
        your Spirit came
        and with it,
            my heart grew restless.
My days were filled with questions,
        visions,
        dreams of a calling beyond my life
        in this religious order.
Could you be calling *me*?
        Can this be *your* voice I hear?
        But why? And to what do you call me?

You have helped me to be free,
        free enough to say good-bye
        to friends I loved deeply,
            friends I loved tenderly,
            friends with whom I prayed,
                cried
                and shared meals.

I knew part of me would die
    in this leave-taking
    so another part of me could live.
Yet from the loss
    you resurrected new life.
I don't know what lies before me
    yet I know you're leading me.
I feel like a child
    in those first swimming lessons,
        walking out on that long diving board.
I was afraid to jump off
    even though I knew
    my teacher was waiting there
        to catch me
        and keep me safe.

I've many unanswered questions, God:
    Who will be there
        to catch me now?
    Who will share my journey to your heart?
        Who will pray with me,
            understand me,
            and know me
            as these friends have?
    And what if I'm wrong?
        (O God, could I be wrong?)
        Who will support me then?
            Help me pick up and keep going?
            Stand with me,
                even in darkness?
I trust you'll be with me
    in all of this.
I trust I'll find your love
    in the new people
    and the new places
        to which I'm now going.

I believe that nothing,
    not even this choice,
    despite what others may say,
        nothing can separate me
            from your love.
If you desire one thing for me, Lord,

it is my freedom,
freedom as a child of God.
You've revealed the truth of a new direction
and that truth has set me free;
trusting this Spirit
I now leap into unknown territory.
A golden chapter in my life
comes to an end
as a new one begins.
Thank you for this wonderful,
awe-filled
and mysterious new beginning.

# A Priest Reflects
# on His Decision
# to Leave Active Ministry

You have no idea
    what it means to be alone
    until you're ordained a priest.
I didn't.

1973 was the year
    I lost myself
    and became someone else.
On my ordination day,
    (or two days before it
    for my Aunt Emma)
        people stopped calling me
        by name.
They started calling me
    "Father."
It was "Father this..."
    and "Father that..."
        but never just "Herb."
No one ever called me Herb any more,
    except other priests
    and not even all of them.
Even my mother started calling me
    Father. I know she was proud
    to have a son in the priesthood
        but still....
Some people even stopped talking to me
    directly at all,
    like you couldn't talk directly
        to a priest.
So a woman would come to the rectory door
    and speak to me like this:
    "Does Father want some vegetables
        from my garden?" she'd ask.
You know, the whole thing in the third person

like I wasn't there
and someone else was living in my body.
I felt like saying,
  "No, Father doesn't;
    but Herb would love some!"


It wasn't just my name I lost, though;
  I also lost other things,
    like color.
I mean, I have nothing particular against black
  but is it the only color
  they could have chosen?
Black is beautiful and I wear it now
  because I like its fashion and look,
  but to wear it as a way of saying
    "color is worldly
    and I'm above all that..."
      got old very quickly.
Clothing is one of the ways
  we express ourselves,
  our identity.
It's a choice we make each day
  that I rarely made at all.
I always felt the people in the parishes
  where I served
  never knew me until they saw
    my Hawaiian shirt
    but the bishop in this diocese was clear:
      he wanted us in black.
He made it sound like a matter
  of holy obedience or something...
  ...so black it was.


I also lost my home;
  I don't care how you decorate it
  or dress it up,
    a rectory is a rectory
    and I lived in a rectory.
It was my office really,
  secretaries and volunteers running
    all over the house
    and, I mean,
      it was *their* house.

It belonged to the parish,
     of course.
But sometimes a guy just wants to go downstairs
     in his underwear
     (or maybe in nothing at all!)
     to get a beer or whatever.
Not in that rectory:
     never.


I also lost my free time,
     almost completely.
I fought hard to keep a day off but
     with so few priests
     and so much work,
          the expectations were there
          and I hated to say no
          and the minute I thought I was done,
               the phone would ring
               and I'd be off to the hospital.
I was really "on call" 24 hours a day.
     Just try telling someone
     who calls with a death in the family:
          "I'm sorry, I'm on my day off today.
          Could you call back
               tomorrow?"


I was paid a pittance
     for this duty
     so that even on my day off,
          I really stayed in the rectory
          most of the time.
Some of the other priests
     had family inheritances
     but my family died old and poor
          and I had very little.
So I stayed in the rectory
     or got together with other priests
     or watched some television
          or sometimes worked on a hobby
          which is what my spiritual director
               recommended.


As a priest, I was

a public representative of the church
and I took the rap
> for whatever the pope was saying
> this week.

Over the years as a priest
> I was blamed for Rome's decisions:
>> not to ordain women,
>> not to sell its art treasures,
>> not to accept homosexuals,
>> not to permit outdoor weddings(!),
>> not to permit birth control,
>> not to allow divorce,
>> not to put Latin back in the Mass
>> not to encourage Benediction,
>> not to do whatever this liberal
>>> or that conservative
>>>> wanted....

To tell you the truth,
> I got sick of it all.

I didn't want to defend Rome sometimes
> but sometimes I did
> and I felt confused and angry
>> about being in the middle.

I'd get orders from the bishop
> to do this
> or not to do that
>> and often I didn't even believe in it
>> but I still had to do it.

"Obedience," I'd think,
> I have to obey.
> So I preached against birth control,
>> for pro-life,
>> against homosexuals,
>> for the annual appeal,
>> against divorce,
>> for a special retirement collection,
>> against women altar servers.

For God's sake!
> I was always in the middle.

And to top it off,
> I was working in a system
> which believed only the priest could do things
>> that ordinary Catholics

could do just as well.
The system was so heavily invested
        in ordination
        that baptism was almost an afterthought.
Today the organizing sacrament of the church
        is clearly ordination
        which places the burden squarely
                on the shoulders of the priests
                which is just where it doesn't belong.
Today we ordain as if it were everything
        and baptize as if it were nothing!

Most of the people in the parishes I served
        weren't *forming* church,
        they were *joining* church
                the same way you join
                a country club,
                except the dues at church were less.

And that's another thing,
        money.
God, how I hated the budget!
        In our diocese if there was a priest
                who couldn't raise money
                they thought your ordination was invalid!
I mean,
        we raised money for the parish,
                for the school,
                for the bishop,
                for the missions,
                more for the bishop!
                        but what about the poor?
                        what about abused women?
                        what about AIDS ministry?
That was a tough part for me
        and when people ask me what I miss least
        I always say, "raising all that damn money."

And on top of all this,
        every time I read about the priesthood
        in the newpapers,
                it had to do with sexual misconduct.
I'll tell you the truth:

I was embarrassed sometimes
to say I was a priest.
But beyond that,
I felt so much pain for my brother priests
who were obviously falling apart
and no one was doing anything about it.
I mean,
these guys were suffering!
Overworked,
underpaid,
blamed for the church's problems,
living in their offices,
paid a pittance,
called by their titles,
dressed only in black:
who in his right mind
would want such a job?
I'll tell you who:
mostly conservative young men
who want to restore the "old" priesthood.
A lot of the guys who want this job
are those who plan to make it into something
for themselves.
Even the ones who come into it
with high hopes,
good training,
and hearts full of love for people,
will be trapped in the impossible,
trapped in a system
that kills priests.
They'll become mired down
in a priestly caste created
for the seventeenth century
but rapidly losing credibility
and viability
in today's world.

And, despite the difficulties
of the living conditions,
the social standing,
and the endless amount of work,
I was asked to do it alone,
with no mate or companion.

I was asked to be celibate
>> on top of it all.
Celibacy isn't just "not being married,"
>> it's also not being touched tenderly,
>> not sharing a life,
>> not coming home to anyone.
A lot of folks are single
>> and many of them are celibate
>> so priests aren't the only ones.
But for the priest,
>> it isn't even acceptable to develop
>>> close friendships,
>>> the kind of "daily friends"
>>>> who stay in touch
>>>> with your life.
To be seen in public with a woman
>> or a man
>> too often
>>> was to invite criticism.
She'd be seen as my mistress,
>> or he as my boyfriend.
Who can win?
>> Most priests give up.
>> They often live alone
>>> and watch a lot of television,
>>>> or work too hard,
>>>> or drink too much,
>>>> or "marry" a hobby of some kind.
Or they engage in secret sexual liaisons
>> without commitment,
>> or, worse yet,
>>> engage in sexual misconduct
>>> with children or the vulnerable.

So I began to consider my original commitment
>> in light of my frustrations,
>>> my anger,
>>> my loneliness,
>>> and my disappointment.
I began to think about what God wants
>> for me
>> for the church
>> and for the world.

To my way of discerning,
      if I really wanted to serve God
      and at the same time be a healthy man,
            I should leave the priesthood
                  and get a job
                        implementing the Gospel's values
                            in our society.
I should teach the faith,
      lead prayer,
      and preside at meetings
            where people give more than lip service,
            where they're really *forming*
                  the community of Jesus
                  in today's world.
And at the same time,
      I should develop a lifestyle
      that is balanced and healthy,
            one that offers me work and rest,
            time alone and time with others,
            committed love, if that's my calling,
            and committed ministry.
I should trust my inner voices,
      clarified in spiritual direction,
      and made more clear yet
            by prayer and retreat time,
            by talking with friends and family,
            and by an open dialogue
                  with my bishop.

              *Pause*

I did finally leave the priesthood,
      four years ago
      and you know,
            I realize now
            that I loved being a priest.
I loved being there
      at those crucial moments
      in people's lives.
I loved sharing the spiritual journeys,
      loved the preaching,
      especially loved the Eucharist.
What I didn't love

was how they forced me to live,
what they forced me to do
to stay.
I was selling my soul then
and when I realized I was unhealthy
and the system, too,
I had no choice but to go.
My inner sense of this,
my intuitions,
led me to that surely and confidently.
I know I did what was right
but I do have some sorrow
about it yet.
If they'd let me,
I'd go back now
and work again in that ministry,
but married priests
aren't welcome.
Don't get me wrong,
I enjoy my work now very much
and I believe I'm annoucning
the Reign of God.
I'm just a little sad,
that's all,
that the church I love so much
won't accept me as a priest
because I also love a spouse.
I'm sad it doesn't love me enough
to rejoice in my happiness
and to support my more balanced life.
I'm delighted for the guys
who find this their real home,
who can cope with the stress
and come out singing!
But I'm sad for some of my brother priests
who remain in their parishes,
and who live lives of desperation,
overwork,
and loneliness.
I'm just a little sad about it,
that's all.

Part Four

# Women

# The Fundamental Catholic Problem with Women
# Is Not One Shared
# by Jesus or the Gospels

The trouble with females,
        as modern "bio-theologians" can tell you,
        is that they're not male.
The official position of the church
        regarding the full inclusion of women
                seems to have that as its argument:
                        "Women are fine
                        but they're simply not men."
Jesus, it seems,
        preferred men,
        and, apparently,
                celibate ones at that.
Therefore, the argument runs,
        women cannot be included
        because they weren't chosen by Jesus.
Furthermore,
        women do not "resemble" Jesus
        which is to say
                they do not have
                the kind of male body Jesus did.
Even though this sounds too simple,
        what other argument
        could the official church
                possibly be making
                by its refusal to include women?
Surely they couldn't mean
        women don't resemble Jesus
        in their souls!
And surely they couldn't mean
        women don't resemble Jesus

in their spirits!
And *surely* they could never have meant
        that women do not resemble Jesus
        in their relationship to God!
The only way,
        in fact,
        that women do not resemble Jesus
            in his pre-Resurrection life,
            is biologically.

According to the argument
        of these church officials,
        Jesus was the first bishop,
        and he ordained the Twelve.
He chose them,
        according to this line of thinking,
        because they were men
            like himself.
He was, they would argue,
        making a *biological* choice.
So women can't be ordained
        because their biology is all wrong,
            or so the argument goes....

It's time for an end
        to this foolish thinking.
It's time for us to take this
        into our own hands
        as responsible adult followers of Jesus
            and, once and for all,
            agree together
            that Jesus did indeed choose women.
And then we should start ordaining
        the women who prepare and present themselves,
        the ones acknowleged by a community
            to be fit leaders,
            and we should do so now.
If the bishops won't,
        then the rest of us should
        just do it ourselves.
We should act as responsible
        communities of faith
        and call them forth

and lay our corporate hands on them
to ordain them ourselves.
And we should do the same thing
for married people
who are ready for ordination, too.


In the first place,
the essential sacerdotal sacrament
of the church isn't ordination.
It's baptism.
That is to say,
the essential sacrament for ministry,
for becoming holy guides,
servants,
and witnesses to one another
is baptism.
Ordination is only an enlargement of baptism.
It's an office in the church,
meant to provide "holy order" there
but not meant to be thought
the end-all of ministry.
If women aren't capable of being ordained,
a relatively minor sacrament,
then they shouldn't be baptized either!


In the second place,
the Gospels do not include any account
of a first-century ordination ceremony
at which anyone was present,
let alone solely men.
The Last Supper is an account of a meal,
not an ordination rite.
The Gospels do not present a sacramentary,
setting down Jesus' intentions
for the priesthood of the church today.
They are not a source
from which we can draw such details.
We assume a great deal about the Gospel
when we assume that Jesus intended
an all-male priesthood such as we have today.
We assume too much,
I fear.

And in the third place,
>>it is becoming more and more plain to us
>>that women did take a significant role
>>>in the early church
>>>and that the truth about this
>>>has been hidden for centuries.
The texts of extra-biblical documents
>>only recently discovered and translated
>>or only recently obtained
>>>from closed libraries,
>>>suggests that women and men
>>>worked together as leaders
>>>until patriarchy began to dominate.

In short,
>>our reasons for not including women
>>>are built on sand,
>>>not on rock.
The plain and simple truth is
>>that we do not ordain women
>>because we have failed to accept redemption.

Redemption was not foisted upon us
>>by the life and death of Jesus
>>but is realized slowly
>>>as we grow more and more
>>>toward Paradise.
Paradise is what we're created for
>>and what grace now leads us back to.
We're created as partners
>>with one another
>>and with Earth.
That's the story of Genesis:
>>*men and women are created*
>>*as partners.*
Earth is a balanced order of life:
>>inter-dependent
>>and fragile.
Procreation itself teaches us this.
>>No one can procreate alone.
The feminine and masculine spirits
>>intermingle and mix
>>within us and around us

to make us whole,
which is to say,
to provide salvation.
"Salvation" is a word of Latin origin
which means, literally,'
"to be made whole," or
"to be restored to full life."
Karl Jung spoke of the anima and animus,
the joining of the feminine and masculine within us
which leads to psychological balance.
As we re-discover this today,
we realize it is of God's own doing
that the feminine and masculine
be partnered.
Jesus himself made this more than abundantly clear
which is why the argument
that he preferred males
is frivolous.
Jesus partnered with many women
as his friends and companions.
The remnants of the stories
of Jesus' life
which the Gospels give us
are filled with these details.
Despite heavy first-century patriarchy
in both society and religion,
these details survived
because, we surmise,
they were so prominent
in Jesus' practices.
We also have
the recently discovered
Nag Hammadi texts to support this.
Jesus broke down the anti-feminine
social barriers
of that historical period
which prevented men, especially rabbis,
from including women.
Jesus was alone with women who weren't relatives
which was taboo behavior
in the first century.
He often touched women,
even ones who were bleeding,

and was touched himself by them
and all of it was forbidden behavior
in those times and places.
Jesus abolished those barriers
to the Reign of God.
He abolished in his own actions,
intentions,
and person
the artificial patriarchal barriers
between women and men.
I believe he hoped
they would be abolished forever.
But in our own time
we seem to have found an argument
to undo Jesus' hopes and dreams for us
in this regard
by excluding women from ministry.

Furthermore, we assume Jesus' celibacy;
we assume he never married,
but why?
Is it that we can't imagine him
"tainting" himself
by loving and being with a woman
in intimate tenderness?
Nowhere does the Gospel tell us
that Jesus said anything about celibacy,
that he approved or disapproved,
or even cared.
We should not assume
that Jesus avoided women
but rather we should assume he loved them
just as he did men.

The Gospel accounts also tell us
that Jesus was supported financially
by women,
that he depended upon them.
They tell us that many women
traveled with Jesus,
taking in his teachings and
(we must assume this)
being sent out by him

among the 72 in Luke 10.
His teaching on divorce,
    is pro-woman:
    men cannot simply trade women
        like property,
        like cattle or oxen,
    for women, like men, are sacred persons.


And the Gospel's agree on this:
    at the highpoint of the story of Jesus,
    the point on which the ending turns,
        the Resurrection,
        it was women who first recognized Jesus.
In fact,
    only Mary of Magdala
    was present, for example,
    in John's Gospel,
        at the death,
        the burial,
        *and* the tomb on Easter morning.
All the Gospels agree.
    It was Mary Magdalene and other women to whom
    the Risen Lord first appeared.
And where were the men?
    Hiding like cowards
    and unwilling to believe
        that Jesus had chosen Mary first.
And today's churchmen are still unwilling
    to admit that *Jesus chooses women.*
        Period.


Doesn't all this suggest strongly
    that Jesus included women
    and chose them
    and loved them?
Doesn't all this suggest strongly
    that Jesus' actions and life
    sought to break any social barriers
    to the full inclusion of women?
And doesn't it suggest
    that the imposition
    of a male-dominated and controlled clergy
        *blasphemes* the Spirit of Jesus?

In reflecting on this situation
    in the church today
    there is only one conclusion
        I can reach:
Our colossal failure to recognize,
    accept,
    develop,
    and integrate women
        and the feminine spirit,
        is a failure to accept redemption.

# A Girl Talks
# About Her First Practice
# as an Altar Server

I wanted to be
      an altar server.
Mrs. Franklin, my fouth-grade teacher,
      announced that training
      for new altar servers
      would begin next Wednesday
         after school
         for anyone interested.

I was so excited!
      I'd waited all through third grade
      because I knew I wasn't old enough yet.
On the bus ride home
      I asked Patty,
      my best friend,
         if she was going to be
         an altar server, too.
She said she didn't know we could.
I said, "Why not?
      Of course we can,
      if we want to."
When I got home,
      I skipped up the driveway;
      my plaid skirt skipping with me.
I was so happy to tell mom.
      I opened the front door
      and unlaced my shoes.
Mom was already busy making supper.
      She asked why I had
      such a big grin on my face.
I told her
      I was going to be an altar server
      and that next week
         was the first meeting.
I was beaming!

She chuckled as she stirred
      the pot on the stove,
      a wooden spoon in her hand.
"Honey, you can't be an altar server."
      She didn't even look up
          from her work.
          This was obviously a matter of fact
             to her....
"Why not?" I asked,
      feeling like a popped balloon.

"Because you're a girl," she said,
      "and they don't let girls
          be altar servers."

"Why not?" I asked again.
"Because they don't allow little girls
      near the altar.
      Only boys can be altar servers."

And with that
      she sent me upstairs
      to start my homework.
I ran up the stairs
      and closed my door.
          I didn't want anyone
          to see me crying.
I laid on my bed
      and untied my pony tail.
Who doesn't want me
      near the altar?
          I thought.
My mom must be wrong.
      Fr. Adams?
      Why wouldn't he want me near the altar?
Or is it Sr. Elizabeth?
      Is she the one
          who doesn't want me
          to be an altar server?

Is it God?
      It must be God!
God doesn't want me near the altar.

I began to cry again.
        I didn't understand
        why only boys could be altar servers
                and not girls.
Does God love boys more than girls?
        I made up my mind
        that God would never have favorites
                like that
                and my mom must be wrong.
                        She *must* be!
So I secretly decided I would go
        to the meeting next Wednesday.

The week passed slowly.
        As the clock neared 3:00
                on Wednesday afternoon,
                I could feel the butterflies
                        in my stomach.
I walked down the hall toward the church,
        afraid to go in.
I hid behind the bulletin board,
        and watched Joel and Tommy go in.
                Brian was no more
                than a few steps behind.
But there were no girls! Maybe mom was right.

I reluctantly opened the door to the church
        and walked in.
The meeting had already begun.
        Fr. Adams was up front with about
        fifteen boys in the first pews.
I started walking
        toward the front of the church;
        my heart was pounding.
Fr. Adams looked up and asked,
        "What are you doing here, Stacy?"
The big booming voice echoed
        and filled the silent church.
"I'm here to be an altar server,"
        I replied shyly.
"I'm sorry," the voice said,
        "this is only for the boys."
A chorus of laughter rose

from the front pews
    and I,
    I froze in fear;
    the laughter seemed to grow
        louder and louder.

I turned and ran from the church
    and the cruel laughter.
The playground
    was my sanctuary
    and I sat there and sobbed.
"Why can't I be an altar server?" I thought.
    "It's only because I'm a girl."
I hated Fr. Adams
    and those boys
    who laughed at me.
Why should it matter that I'm a girl?
    They wear those long white robes
    that look like dresses anyway.
I could cut my hair short,
    and then no one would notice
        I was a girl.
Maybe God *does* have favorites,
    I finally realized,
    and, apparently,
        none of them are girls
        like me.

# A Man Reveals
# His First Experience
# With a Woman

At some point I could have told you
           this would happen.
At some point
           I knew inside I would finally
           encounter a woman.
It happened last Sunday.

There is an open and affirming
           ecumenical church in our community,
           one that welcomes and affirms
                      the many folks on the margins
                      of mainline Christian churches.
I went there last week
           with a friend of mine
           to whom this congregation
                      has become very important.
He'd been asking me to go with him
           and I admit I'd avoided it
           but finally his persistence
           overcame my fears
                      and off we went.

This church doesn't have much money;
           or maybe they spend their money
           on things other than their building.
They meet in an old warehouse,
           painted well and decorated nicely
           but folding chairs take the place of pews
           and the space in which the chairs sit
                      for the service
                      quickly becomes the social hall
                      at the end of the worship.
Nonetheless, the place was filled
           with hugging, warm, and friendly people.

It was filled with folks
    familiar enough with other churches
    but at home here.
We met his friends
    and we sat with them
    and soon the service began.

I wasn't ready for what happened next,
    not ready at all:
    it was my first experience
        with a woman.
To be greeted there by that feminine voice
    seemed both unfamiliar to my Catholic roots
    and yet so absolutely right.
To the others present,
    I'm sure this was just
    another normal Sunday worship service
        but not to me.
To me it was a beam of light
    shining into the church.
    What I'd argued for,
        and fought for,
        and supported for so long,
        in my own church
            was a normal part of life
            for these people.
Her sermon was her own;
    she was no guest preacher,
    snuck in by the pastor
    without permission from the bishop
        who would have had to say "no,"
        because the pope doesn't permit it.
This was no exception,
    I soon figured out.
This woman is a minister,
    a full,
    ordained,
    obviously gifted minister.
She has taken her place
    among the other ministers
    without respect to gender.
And it seemed so right to me,
    so perfectly right,

I sat there in my chair,
        filled simultaneously
        with shock and delight!
I sat there with tears creeping around my eyes,
        wetting my cheek.
I sat there wondering why
        the women of my own tradition
        were so feared by the men in charge.
I sat there numbed by the balance,
        beauty,
        and grace of this charmed worship.
"From time to time,"
        she was saying in her sermon,
        "since I have been your co-pastor,
        I have chosen to sit with you during communion
            rather than be a server.
I do this so that I will remember who we are
        as a community of faith.
It's a blessing to sit and sing
        and behold us
        as we come forward in every configuration
                to receive the bread of life
                and the cup of liberation.
I am always so struck by this..."
        And here she began to weep herself,
        along with me and my friend.
"...struck by the fact that out here on the margins
        we are re-claiming who we are
        as peculiar individuals.
Out here on the margins
        we are re-inventing
        who we are as a community of faith.
Out here on the margins
        we are seeking to extend the possibilities
                of truth between us,
                as we seek to incarnate God among us."

Part Five

# Gay or Lesbian Christians

# Church Teaching
# on Gay or Lesbian Love,
# How It Fits into Discernment

Church teaching on what sexual behavior
        is appropriate
        for gay and lesbian people
            is clear:
            None is permitted.

Gay and lesbian people are judged
        acceptable insofar
        as the orientation itself
            is concerned:
Nothing sinful in being who you are.
        But any sexual activity
        is forbidden.
Gay and lesbian people,
        in the mind of the church,
        are called to celibacy.

The primary basis for this position
        is twofold.
First, gay and lesbian sex
        is considered unnatural
        and second,
            a literal reading of Scripture
            condemns it.
The teaching of the church
        on this matter,
        and on this basis,
            has been consistent
            for many centuries
            and is not likely
                to undergo revision soon.

Certainly,
    it must be noted,
    there is strong disagreement
        about this
        among theologians
            psychologists,
            sociologists,
            and gay and lesbian people.
Nevertheless,
    the teaching of the church
    is firm and clear
    and must be taken into account
        as decisons are made
        about how gay and lesbian people
    will live together.


Dick Westley has provided an excellent
    treatment of how Christians
    can respond to this teaching
    in his *Morality and Its Beyond.*
He urges a pastoral response
    that takes as its first value
    living a life which is at once
        faithful to the Divine Presence
        in Jesus Christ,
        and also true to our human selves.
The primary end of human sexuality,
    he argues,
    is relational, not legal.
It is meant to draw us together,
    not keep us apart.
For him,
    as for the church
    this happens in the context of love.
Spousal love is characterized by
    commitment,
    permanence,
    and exclusivity.
This traditional teaching about marriage applies,
    according to Westley,
    to gay and lesbian
        as well as straight
        couples.

In the meantime,
 gay men and lesbians
 struggle to know how to live as Christians
  and how to reconcile the inner sense
  of what is "natural" for life.
The goodness of procreation
 is a very great value
 in human sexuality,
  but it is not the only value.
Personal dignity,
 committed friendship,
 interpersonal sharing,
 and psychologial health are also values.
But perhaps the greatest value of the Gospel
 is overlooked in this
 as arguments for and against
 gay and lesbian love
  are posed and debated.
The Gospel,
 it seems,
 is clear about this in the mission of Christ:

  God is intent upon
  the transformation of the world
  through Christ,
   the Faithful One
   who knew his inner call
   and responded in love.

  Christ has chosen us
  as workers in this New Community,
   a community of justice,
    peace,
    kindness,
    caring,
    compassion,
     and mercy....

  In this New Community,
  our mission is less
  maintenance of the law
   and more the application of the law
   in such a way

that we can love God freely
and completely
and so love one another
as we do ourselves.


Gay men and lesbians,
like all straight followers of Jesus,
are called to this mission and work
in the New Community.
The first call,
for any sexual person,
is not to love their partners
but to love the Word,
the Source of Life,
the Divine Presence Among Us:
Emmanuel!
Fidelity is always understood
as an expression of covenant:
God's with us,
leading to ours with each other.
The end of this,
however,
is not self-fulfillment in and of itself
but rather that the mission of Christ
be done by us.
So if gay and lesbian couples
join in commitments for life
or if straight ones do,
the purpose is the same:
to make us more selfless,
more able to announce the Good News
that God is Love.
When this end is twisted or ignored
or forgotten and pushed aside
in favor of selfishness
the results will be darkness.
The result will be an endless pursuit of sex
or sexual partners
or hope of permanence
or talk of love
but nothing will satisfy,
nothing!
unless it rests in the Divine Mystery.

This isn't a gay and lesbian reality alone,
>           but one shared
>           by all lovers and spouses
>                   everywhere.
All of us are called to the Divine Mystery.

All of us need companionship
>           and seek long-term friends
>           who can really come to "know" us.
All of us hope to grow old
>           together with those we love.
All of us experience sexual urges,
>           the desire to touch
>                   and be touched by others.

In order to know what God wants for us,
>           we cannot blindly follow
>           either social customs
>                   or church law.
In order to understand God's will
>           we must listen to our hearts,
>           we must *discern* our way.
We discern our way
>           among the competing values
>           and church norms,
>                   among our inner needs and
>                   community responsibilities.
We discern our way
>           because there is no map,
>                   no designated route for each person
>                           to follow....
In this discernment process
>           we must weigh church teaching
>           alongside the Scriptures,
>                   the truth of our own experience
>                   alongside the guidance of others.
In the end,
>           in our souls,
>           we will know the right way for us
>           if we have been faithful to these truths
>                   and earnest in our search.

Listening to the life experiences

of gay and lesbian people
can help us form a consistent ethic and norm
for ourselves
in thinking about this.
The norm seems to be this:
we should welcome commitment,
welcome fidelity to one another,
welcome the celebrations of faith
which result from friendship.
We should welcome, not reject,
stable relationships resulting
in blessed and holy unions of love.
We should welcome, not reject,
the talents,
beauty,
witness,
and signs of divine presence
which gay men and lesbians
provide for us today.

# What Does It Mean
# for Gay or Lesbian People
# to Know Jesus?

We live in times
        that are full of mystery.
The predictable,
        same-as-last-year
        we-know-what's-coming
        this-is-how-people-are
        these-are-the-rules
        times of the past:
                if they really ever existed,
                they no longer do.
Even if at some other time
        in human history,
        before television
        or telephone
        or the airplane—
    or *sometime*—
                life did seem more predictable
                it probably *felt* unpredictable.
Life probably felt uncertain
        in every age.
Every age has brought
        war,
        or famine,
        or new ideas,
        or difficult events.
Every age of history
        is filled with the change
        in which the human family has been engaged:
                outlooks and beliefs
                fashions and styles
                relationships
                the weather

                   family structures
                   religious customs
                   economic systems
                   inner awareness.
Even Earth itself
            is constantly changing.
Sometimes change comes with violence
            and revolution;
            other times more slowly and almost
                   imperceptibly.
Sometimes we hear about it
            because the president or prime minister
            announces it to the press;
                   other times a neighbor mentions
                   it over the fence.
Sometimes we witness crowds
            protesting in the streets
            with pickets and posters;
                   other times it's a silent protest
                   within our own hearts
                          as we do whatever it is
                          our consciences direct.
However we learn about it,
            whatever it is,
            change is the one sure thing,
                   as Marshall McLuhan has said.


Today change is much more fast moving
            than it's been at times in the past:
                   global in scale
                   electronic in speed
                   universal in effect.
It feels difficult to stay informed
            as frontier after frontier
                   is reached
                   explored
                   and shown to the public.
Have we reached the last frontier?
            Probably not.
We thought so when explorers finished
            with Earth
            but then there was the moon.
And in the time since we began sharing ideas

through television and radio,
we have talked publicly and endlessly
          about economics,
                    politics,
                    women's rights,
                    medicine,
                    psychology,
                    sociology,
                    human questions of every kind.
And we have explored our inner lives,
          our private lives:
                    divorce,
                    abortion,
                    family violence,
                    poverty,
                    child abuse,
                    birth control,
                    criminal attitudes,
                    emotional growth,
                    new age religion,
                    and homosexuality.
But of course,
          there's really nothing new in this.
You will find these questions,
          most of them,
          discussed among the Greeks
          400 years before Christ,
                    and before them,
                    among others.
These questions are ageless;
          it isn't so much that they've changed
          as that the speed with which
                    we can dialogue about them
                    as a global human family
                              has changed so dramatically!


Because of this speed,
          this electronic speed,
          it's been difficult
          for thinking people
                    to know what to believe,
                    how to behave,
                    and how to treat those who disagree.

Sometimes our treatment
     of those who are different than us
     has been less than kind,
          sometimes it's been downright mean,
          sometimes it's been vicious.
And it's been especially tough
     for the people of the church
     to know what to do next.
Here change occurs more slowly,
     with more study.
     Sometimes hundreds of years of study
          precedes a single relatively minor change.
"The Tiber," they say,
     "flows very slowly toward the sea...."
Only very grudgingly will Catholic leaders
     agree that some teachings may develop
        over time,
        and that influences
             outside the official church
             may affect theology.
So all this recent change
     and all this speed
     has been particularly troubling
        for church leaders.
These leaders have been able in the past
     to declare something true
     and instruct the faithful how to behave.
The faithful, by and large, went along with this
     and fashioned their lives
     and their families
        on this basis.
I know everyone has heard of families,
     not that long ago,
     where a sister or brother
     was disowned for marrying the wrong person:
        divorced,
        racially wrong,
        non-Catholic
        or non-something!
I know we all know families,
     maybe we are such a family,
     where the decision on birth control
        forced us to choose:

                    Will we be in or out of the church?
I know we have heard of families,
          many of them,
          where a gay or lesbian child
                    is such a source of shame
                    and dishonor
                    that the child is banished.
Such banishment of gay or lesbian children
          is the question
          we want to treat here for a moment.
The banishment might be literally
          an order not to return home
          until "your sinful lifestyle changes..."
                    or simply an emotional distance,
                    a barrier to talking about it,
                    or to meeting friends,
                              or lovers.
Whatever form it takes,
          gay men and lesbians,
          stand on the edge of another frontier
          of human openness and struggle,
                    but they receive no blessing
                    and only a curse
                              from the Community of Jesus today,
                              from the offical church.


There's a story
          in one of the gospels
          which can help us discern
                    what Jesus' regard
                    might have been like
                    toward those bound up
          by death-dealing attitudes and boundaries,
          including gay and lesbian people today.
It's the story of Lazarus
          in chapter 11 of John.
The story begins
          with Jesus and his friends
          going off to an out-of-the-way place
                    to rest.
The church authorites of his day and age
          were on Jesus' case
          because he taught what they refused to see.

There was talk of "doing him in,"
    of "getting rid of him...."
This talk hadn't been lost on him
    —or on his friends,
        who were probably grateful for this chance
            to stay out of sight for a while.

But while he was there in his hiding place
        word came to him that a friend
            was sick: Lazarus.
He decided to return
        to Judea, to Bethany,
            where Lazarus had lived...
                ...and now had died.
He knew he would be
        facing terrible dangers
        if he went.
But he also knew he had no choice:
        Lazarus would be a sign for all
        that Jesus can set anyone free,
                even those in tombs,
                those bound up for death.
So he went,
        over the objections of his followers,
            and maybe even
            despite his own best judgment.
His disciples tried to stop him
        from going
        because they knew the dangers were real.
They didn't want to go through this
        with him,
                didn't want to be hurt themselves,
                didn't want the risks,
                    the public trials,
                    the pain.

"The ones who walk in the light,"
        he told his worried friends,
        "do not stumble.
It's only the ones who remain in the dark
        who need to worry
        about falling down."

I'm not sure this convinced them all
          but off they went,
          returning to Bethany,
          looking for Lazarus,
                    now dead four days
                    and buried in his tomb.
Deeply buried in this story
          is the truth about Jesus
                    and us.
Jesus gives the gift of life
          even at risk of his own,
          the offering of his own life for ours,
          the giving away of Self
                    for the good of others,
                    for the truth.
"Whoever lives and believes in me,"
          he will tell Lazarus's sister,
                    "shall live."
                    Period.
And, as this story goes,
          that's apparently true,
          even for those living,
                    or dying,
                    in a tomb.
In this story,
          Lazarus takes the part of all of us
          who live "tomb lives,"
                    all who are bound up
                    and kept out of sight.
This isn't so much a story
          about a dead man being restored
                    to physical life
                    as about the spiritually dead
                    coming to life in Christ.
This is a story
          about binding up and letting go free,
          about having life,
                    real life,
                    true life in Christ.
It's about us when we come face to face
          with death in life,
          with isolation,
                    rejection,

hiding,
fear,
self-loathing,
and hate.
All of us are Lazarus
      from time to time:
            dead to life
            bound up,
            and buried in a tomb...
                  ...or a "closet."
Gay and lesbian people
      know what this means
      in a profound way.
Like certain others in our time,
      being gay or lesbian today
      can involve a lot of hiding.
It can involve
      a good deal of time spent bound up,
            by attitudes of hate
            by stereotypes of style
            by the denial of love
            by threats of violence.
To be openly gay or lesbian today
      one must be steeled
            for rejection,
            ridicule,
            misunderstanding,
            and danger.
Even those who claim to represent Jesus,
      particpate in this
      and do so
            in the name of God.

But Jesus' assurance is
      that the truth will set us free,
      that acknowledging and living by that truth
            by the Spirit of Truth,
            ushers us into the Reign of God
            announced here by Jesus himself.
And if you listen closely
      to gay men and lesbians today,
            you will hear this chorus:
            "We are who we are."

They are supported in this by
                psychologists,
                sociologists,
                biologists,
                philosophers,
                and many theologians.
Gay men and lesbians will tell you plainly
        that their way of loving
        comes as "naturally" to them
        as straight men and women
                understand their attractions.
Lesbians and gay men will tell you
        that the truth is this:
        sexuality is a gift from God
        and homosexuality is one expression
                of that gift.
That's the truth
        that has set so many
        lesbians and gay men free at last.
That's the truth that has brought them
        out of the closets of hiding,
                out of the tombs.
And in this coming out,
        gay men and lesbians often say that,
        for the first time,
                it is now clear
                how God touches us with eternal truth.


So Jesus' assurance is clear
        when he calls to us
        as he did to Lazarus:
        *"Come out!"*


He isn't calling us out of our graves
        but out of our hiding
        into the light.
He's calling us out of unfreedom
        into freedom.
And, if that isn't clear enough,
        if that doesn't make it obvious
        that we are not made to live in darkness,
                not made to live in closets or tombs,
                Jesus has something else to say.

As the one who had been buried
>> comes stumbling out of the dark,
> still bound,
> still tied up for death,
>>> his hands and feet and face,
>>> Jesus speaks to those around him:
>>> *"Unbind him and let him go!"*

# Why Did You Make Me Gay?

O God,
        why did you do this to me!?
        Why did you create me
            this way?
            Knit me together in my mother's womb
                with this terrible curse?
O God,
        why did you make me gay?

Your promise was to love
        and be with your people,
        to love and be with me!
Do you call this curse
        "being with me"?

Don't you realize
        how much people hate
        and despise me?
Everyone around me
        gets into this with a frenzy!
Haven't you heard the jokes
        and stereotypes
        and condemnations?
On all sides,
        these righteous ones
        instruct me about how to love
            as they do,
            as though their way of love
                is somehow right
                and mine is wrong.

How could you do this
        to me?
        Don't you love me?
Don't you realize
        that even the agents of your church
        reject and hate me?

The church was the one place
    I might have gone
    for comfort,
        the one place where your presence
        might have soothed me and warmed me.
But even there,
    especially there!
    there is no room for me,
    no room for my way of loving.
Church leaders,
    your leaders,
    persecute me constantly,
        calling me names,
        names unfit for any
            of your creation!
They call me "disordered"
        "perverted"
        "sick"
        "evil."
But have I not been ordered this way
    by your very hand?
Have I not
    from birth and
    from earliest childhood
        been called to this
        way of love?
Have you created what is "sick"?
    Is yours a perverted hand?

Did you not promise
    to be with me always;
    did you not say you would stand
        at my side;
        did you not assure me
            to "be not afraid"?
Are you not a faithful God,
    loving and gentle,
    generous and kind?
Are you not inclusive of all?
    Or are you a God
        for those who are "right"
        according to some set of rules
            which do not fit me

and cannot possibly be lived
without denying my very self?
Am I to be gay
but not live that way?
Am I to separate myself from myself,
wrench myself apart
in order to be one way
but love another?
What could you possibly have in mind
for me and my sisters and brothers
who are also gay or lesbian?
Did you give me my sexuality
then order me
to abstain from using it
for love and pleasure?
Are you that cynical, God?
Are you that cruel?
Are you that crazy?
Did you do this to purify me somehow?
to prepare me for your Reign?
Am I supposed to become strong
by withholding sex from myself
and from others?

Am I not supposed to love
with the tenderness I've learned
from you?
Am I not supposed to love
faithfully,
joyfully,
wondrously?

If this is some kind of joke,
O God,
then take it back right now.
If this is a curse from you
with which you want me to suffer,
then come and get it
and take me with it!
If I must hide
and deny
and hate myself
in order to be acceptable

then there is no reason to live.

*Pause*

But...
        there is a reason to live
            for me,
            and that reason is your love.
It comes unconditonally
        and without cost.
It finds me where I am,
        wherever I am,
        and is insistent
                that I am good
                and created by you.
What mystery there is in this!
        What profound mystery!


In your own hidden and wonderful way,
        you have brought me into being
        as a sign of your love.
Even when those around me claim
        I am only a mistake,
                an error of chance
                or worse,
                        "disordered,"
        yet do I know I am ordered according
        to your love.
Even when those around me cannot see you
        within my life
        or my loving,
                yet I know you are there, indeed.
Even when those around me
        claim a corner on the market
        of your revelation,
                yet I know you are revealed in me
                and my sisters and brothers
                        who are gay or lesbian, too.
And even when those around me
        fail to notice your beauty in me,
        or fail to embrace your mystery in me,
                yet do I know of it
                and share it abundantly.

We are signs of your love
>> and only those who cannot see love
>> cannot see that.
We are a sign that challenges others
>> a sign of sameness
>> a sign of continuity
>> a sign of deep and profound
>>>> brotherly and sisterly love.


I stand on the margins of your people
>> as a leper
>> but can see more clearly from these margins
>>>> than from the center.
I can see the narrowness
>> of the too-top-down church
>> and the exclusion and hatred
>>>> of a too-nervous-about-sin-to-see-beauty
>>>> hierarchy.
I can see the fear of the
>> too-much-concern-about-sex magisterium
>> and the prejudice of the
>>>> too-different-from-me public.


I pray that our own
>> too-hurt-to-forgive attitudes
>> and too-promiscuous-to-learn-love habits
>>>> may yield to love.
I pray that we may all become lovers,
>> not haters,
>> all become accepting
>>>> not rejecting.
I pray that you and I
>> can forgive those who hate me
>> and other gay and lesbian folks
>>>> because they do not know
>>>> that in hating us,
>>>>>> they are hating you.

# A Gay Man Can't Believe
# What He Reads in the Papers

I read it in the newspapers
> but I just couldn't believe it.
In fact, it took me a while to focus
> on the headline:
> "Bias Against Gays Encouraged
> > in Vatican Statement."
My eyes seemed to blur for a moment
> and my head was swimming.
> It had to be a mistake in meaning.
Surely this meant the Vatican had finally
> decided to *support* our rights
> as lesbian and gay people!
I must have read the headline wrong
> in that paper.
Surely it couldn't be
> that the Vatican meant gay and lesbian folks
> should become victims of discrimination.
The Vatican is supposed to speak for Christ,
> the light of the world,
> the source of mercy and justice,
> the one who stood in the margins
> > of the church of his own day
> > and argued for tolerance,
> > > kindness,
> > > and inclusivity.
The church wouldn't now be speaking
> in the name of darkness, would it?
> by calling for discrimination to be *increased*
> > rather than eliminated?
Could they really mean
> it's acceptable and even *required*
> for bishops and other Catholics
> to prevent gay and lesbian people
> > from having access to housing
> > or jobs

> or health care
> or families with children?
They hadn't done that
> with divorced and re-married folks
> —and thank God.
They hadn't done it with former priests
> now married without permission
> —and thank God.
They hadn't done so with murders,
> or rapists
> or war-makers
> > so *surely* this couldn't be right!

And even if it was right
> they couldn't mean me.
I mean, I've been a loyal son of the church
> for my entire life.
I've loved and fought for the church,
> defended it when defense seemed impossible,
> > taught her truths,
> > nursed her wounds
> > even scrubbed her floors.
I've retreated her youth,
> sung her songs,
> marched in her processions,
> preached in her churches,
> given myself and my all.
I have really *loved* this church.

Surely they couldn't mean after all that,
> now they would encourage society
> to ban me from security in my housing,
> > or from adopting a child
> > or getting custody after divorce
> > or keeping a job as a teacher
> > or any of the rest.
They just couldn't mean that;
> not about me,
> and not about my gay brothers
> > and lesbian sisters
> > whom I know only as people of love
> > and not as people of hate.

So I read the article
    and re-read it
    and then I cut it out and put it on my desk
        and yesterday I read it again.
It was sinking in.

*I was exactly the one they meant,*
    me and others like me.
We couldn't be trusted, it said,
        couldn't be considered well or healthy,
        couldn't be given rights.
I wonder if they realize how far away they are
        from the world's psychiatric societies
        and others who no longer consider this
            a mental illness.
I wonder if they understand the stereotypes
        they encouarge and believe
        when they connect being gay to being a pedophile.

I wonder if those men in the Vatican know
        how much this will fuel the bashers:
            in courtrooms
            and on the streets.
I wonder if they know how many of their own members
        they're talking about,
        including bishops and priests.
I wonder if they care about the pain
        and agony
        gay and lesbian Catholics are caught in by this.
I wonder if they realize
        what this does to my guts.
I wonder if they realize they are pushing me out
        maybe for good this time.
        Me, and many others like me.

My only fear is that they *do know,*
        they *do* understand all this.
My fear is that my leaving
        is exactly what they want.

So tonight I'm thinking about all these years
        of being with this Church
        and loving her through thick and thin.

And a great and awesome sadness fills me;
> this is my home
> and it will always be my home
>> even when I'm not welcome here
>> and no longer come to visit
>>> —or to pray.

Leaving will not be easy,
> just like a spouse
> in an addictive or abusive home.

I have stayed for so long
and tolerated so much of the church's violence:
> I've been emotionally
>> and verbally abused.
> I've been judged and condemned
>> with no chance for dialogue;
>> no opportunity even to tell my story.
> In a word, I've been "beaten up"
>> and when I screamed for help
>> all the pastors and bishops were silent,
>> all but a few brave ones
>> who were then systematically punished
>>> and run out of their jobs
>>> for standing up for us.
> I've been punched in the stomach
>> and had the air knocked out of me
>> so many times I'm afraid
>>> to even look at the Catholic press
>>> for fear another negative statement
>>> about us will be there.
> And now I've been picked up bodily
>> and thrown against the doors,
>> the *outside* doors of the Church.

They didn't explicitly yell, "Get out, damn it!"
> but they might as well have.

See you around.

# One Man Sings
# of His Love for Another

When I am old
  I shall love you no less fiercely
    than I do now.
I shall run my same hand
  along your back,
  down to where you like me to pause,
  rubbing gently before going on
    and I shall do this
    with no less passion
      and desire
      than I do it today.
I shall gaze at you,
  whether you are sensible or not,
  gaze into your beautiful eyes,
    looking into the same soul
    I do now.

We shall walk then
  as we do now,
    swaying,
    laughing,
  never ending our conversation
  of life and love.
We shall still be talking
  of Heidegger
  and still be wondering
  about moonlandings and moonbeams
    and the winter solstice.
I shall listen then
  as closely as I do now,
  never quitting my longing
    for your voice,
    never leaving behind your sound,
      even when you make that sound
      no more.

I shall sit then
  on this same chair,
  watch you in this same way
    that I do now.
I shall never end
  my watching you,
  noting your eyebrow make its furl,
  seeing your teeth all white when smiling.
I shall never tire
  of your lips
  and never forget
  where they have kissed me.
I can feel them even now
  upon my back
  as you curl around me,
  your arm laying across my chest
    from behind
    holding me in sleep.
Would that we could lie in eternity
  that way,
  you with your arm around me
    from the backside,
    laying across my chest.


When we are old
  we shall have no less time
  than we do now,
    only a moment,
    all in a single moment,
      to say it
      and do it
      and be it with each other.
We will take the copper cookware
  from its shelves then
  and the wooden spoons
  and good knives
    and slice the garlic
    and porcini mushrooms.
And we shall smell those smells,
  not of food
  but of us cooking for one another
    just as we do now.
The food shall be no better then,

it shall taste no better
than it does now
    when we sit across from one another,
    holding dinner parties for two,
        talking big talk
        and small talk
        all at once
        as we continue the theme
            of asking
            and knowing
            and carrying one another's lives.

But shall they still hate us then?
    Shall those who hate us now
        still threaten to kill us then
        for appearing to love in ways
            they cannot know?
Shall we still be cautious
    when going out,
    careful not to look like lovers,
    careful not to touch
        or kiss
        in public?
Shall hate still have its day then,
    when we are old lovers?
Or will our constant,
    steady love
    not prove hate wrong
    and soften the hearts of them
        whose hearts cannot
        bear love?

# A Thirty-Something Lesbian Tells How She Learned About Love

When I was growing up
    my life was really "the pits."
A small town in a rural place
    with very little of anything much:
    that was my home town.
"Libertyville," they called it,
    but there wasn't much liberty,
    not for me anyway.
We were a company town
    because we had one company:
    one that moved out from the City
        and pretty much decided
        what happened in our town.
If the company bosses didn't,
    then the union bosses did.
They made parts for cars:
    axles I think,
    and most of the local men worked there.
It was good money for the town,
    nothing else would have kept it alive.
But that didn't change life:
    it only got 'em all together
    so they could work all day
        and drink all night.
We were what the sociologists call "blue collar"
    and economists call "middle class."
Lots of television,
    beer,
    polyester,
    and gossip:
        that's what they called "Libertyville."

Sometimes I think they named it that
    just to fool the people who live there
    into thinking they're free.

We moved there when I was 10,
>    from another company town
>    in another state.
We lived a hollow life
>    in a hollow house:
>    we came and went
>>        and came and went
>>        but we never really met.
My parents fought a lot:
>    almost every day.
>    They fought about everything:
>>        money mostly,
>>        and about us kids
>>        and about dad's drinking.
I was just a little girl then
>    but I can still remember some of their fights.
Dad would start drinking booze
>    and mom would be smoking
>    and pouring coffee down her like a flood.
She'd be wired and he'd be drunk
>    and the two of them would get into it
>    and hollar and cuss
>>        and us kids,
>>        we just stayed out of the way.
"Out of the way":
>    that kind of summarizes how I lived as a kid.

When I was 14, though,
>    things changed for me
>    because that's when I met Cindy Lincoln.
She was 16, older than me by 2 years,
>    but she liked me
>    and she really took me in.
She took me places
>    and got me out of the hell hole
>    my parents called our home.
We didn't really do anything that special
>    but we were friends
>    and it didn't matter.
Sometimes we'd play softball
>    with the boys in the neighborhood.
>>        (They weren't too good
>>        and we beat 'em all the time.)

Sometimes we went fishin',
        sometimes we hid in her room
        and looked at pictures
                or sewed
                or just sat together and talked.
See, it didn't matter
        what we did
        as long as we did it together.
She'd braid my hair for me,
        and rub my shoulders
        and lay her head against my back.
And sometimes we'd just "start thinkin'."
        You ever done that?
        Just "start thinkin' "?
It'd happen down by the river a lot:
        we'd be walkin' and talkin'
        and then we'd sit and chat a little
        but then suddenly,
                like there was some signal,
                we'd both just go quiet
                and sit there,
                        not movin'
                        not stirrin' a bit:
                        and we'd just "start thinkin'."
I loved those moments best:
        the two of us there
        sittin' by the river,
        smellin' the swamps and fishy river smell,
        nobody to bother us
                and nothin' to say
                but plenty of being together.
I've always felt since that time
        that I'd know I was in love
        because that'd happen to me again:
                someone and me
                would just "start thinkin'"
                and I'd know she was the one for me.
Cindy and me were happy as larks
        that summer.

But then one day,
        a day I'll never forget,
        the sky fell on me.

Dad came home and for once
        he was sober.
The company he worked for,
        he told us,
        was asking him to move to another town
                in another state.
He was getting another promotion
        and mom was ecstatic.
"We'll finally get out of this dump,"
        she said waiving her arm around the room
        and motioning toward town.
"The Ugly Days of Libertyville
        is finally over," she said.
And my two little brothers
        were happy, too.
Partly they were happy because mom and dad
        weren't fighting about this.
And partly they figured
        any move away from the pain of this mess
        would be an improvement.

And I was speechless, too.
        I sat there with my family and listened
        and was happy for dad,
                but I was in another world.
I'd been hit with a hammer
        and suddenly I was awake:
        I'd been sleeping or dreaming
            and I didn't realize what was happening
            with me and Cindy.
But this grotesque announcement woke me up:
        Cindy and I were in love.
I hadn't realized it,
        not fully,
        not consciously,
            until that very moment.

But how could this be?
        She was another girl,
        just like me.
Love can't happen that way:
        it has to be with a girl and a guy.
        That's how it works:

at least in Libertyville.
You see, I'd never even heard the word "gay"
    and I thought the word "lesbian"
    was one of those dirty words
        mom scolded us for using.
All the girls in my class:
    they had their hair done
    and their eyes lined
    and their boyfriends in tow
        but that was never "right" for me.
        I never wanted anyone but Cindy.


But, you see,
        none of this hit me
        until dad came home and said it was over
            and we'd be moving.
We had two weeks.
The company was buying the house
        and dad was leaving next week
        and we were following soon.
They needed him and they wanted him now.


I flew out of the house
        and ran all the way to hers.
She took one look at my face
        and grabbed me and dragged me down the path
            behind the house
            to the river.
She sat me down
        and I sat inside her legs
        and she faced me and I told her.
But here's the amazing part:
        what I understood about her and me
        took form in the very same instant
            the words came bubbling out of my mouth.
As I talked I simultaneously realized
        what I was saying
        and so did she.
We both reached the same conclusion
        in the same instant of our lives:
        and that night, for the first time,
            I knew the ecstacy and joy
                of love.

We didn't have sex:
>we made love
>and I've learned the difference.

We touched and kissed
>and said with our hands and breath and eyes
>what we could never have expressed
>>in a thousand years
>>with our words.

And then we sat up on our blanket
>on that warm August night
>along that old, lazy, summer river
>>when I was 14,
>>and we put our arms around each other
>>>and we just "started thinkin'."

# A Gay Man's Sister Reflects
# on Her Brother's Death from AIDS

I didn't even know he was sick.
      I didn't know.
      Now he's gone.
            Gone...so quickly.
It's so final.

My brother,
      at the age of 26,
          is dead.
There are so many things
      I wish I could change,
      so many things I wish
          I'd have said,
          so many things
             I wish
             I'd have done.
Last week he was alive
      and now six days later,
      his body is lying
      in a casket,
          cold,
          colorless,
          lifeless,
          dead.

I was at work
      when mom called.
She said Matthew
      had been rushed to the hospital,
      that the doctors didn't think
          he'd make it through the afternoon.
I asked, "Why?
      Why?"

Mom didn't say anything.

---

She only wept
        into the phone.
I felt as though someone
        had punched me in the stomach.
My wind,
        my breath,
                was gone.
I ran from my office
        and rushed to the hospital,
        barely able to see the road,
                blinded by the tears
                flowing from my eyes.
When I arrived,
        I could see mom and dad,
        Joanie and Ralph:
                the whole family was there
                        already,
                        standing in the hallway.
But there were others there, too,
        men and women I didn't recognize.
Joanie started toward me.
        We embraced then
        and she sobbed into my shoulder.
I felt confused,
        helpless,
        suddenly very cold,
                very cold.
And I knew then,
        I knew I hadn't arrived
                in time.
Matt was already dead.
        But how could it
                be so? He's my brother;
                        he can't be dead.
                        My tears overwhelmed my hopes
                        and the reality crashed in on me
                                as a vase when it hits the floor.

How long we stood there weeping
        I don't know.
I asked again,
        "Why?
        How?"

None of my family would answer:
        "Mom," I demanded of her,
        "tell me. What's happened to Matt?
            Why is he dead?!"
Still no one would talk.
        I felt frantic,
                and frightened:
                "What's wrong here?
                Why won't anyone tell me
                        what's happening?"


Then one of the men
        who'd been sitting among the others
        came forward
            and touched my arm.
He was a stranger to me
        but his red eyes
        and a face wet with tears
                told me vaguely
                he was connected to Matt.
"Matthew died of Pnuemocystis,"
        he said.
He must have read the confused
        look on my face
        because he explained more:
            "He died of AIDS."
A thunderbolt went off in my body
        somewhere
        and I looked at my mother,
        wondering if she would confirm
                this for me.
She said nothing;
        she wouldn't even look at me.
                And my father: he walked away.


AIDS. He died of AIDS?


I began to weep again,
        somewhere from deep within,
        a river of grief
                began to flow
                out of me...
The man,

the stranger,
>  held me for a moment.
"I'm David,"
>  he told me;
>  "I'm a friend of Matt's."

I walked into his room.
>  The nurses were taking out
>  his IVs.
I saw his body lying there,
>  he looked as though he were sleeping.
How long had it been
>  since I'd last seen him?
>  I didn't even know.

I just stood there
>  and shook
>  and cried.
David came up behind me
>  and I felt his arm come around me.
>  I turned and he took me into his arms
>  >  and I stood there,
>  >  >  trembling and sobbing,
>  >  >  with only the comfort of a stranger
>  >  >  because my family, Matt's family,
>  >  >  >  was silent
>  >  >  >  and absent.

*Pause*

I'm sitting here at his wake now,
>  numb,
>  numb all over.
There are so many people here I don't know,
>  obviously friends of Matt's,
>  friends I've never met,
>  >  people about whom he never talked.
I've never heard of them
>  because I've never asked.
I was never actively part
>  of his life.
After he told me he was gay,
>  I said that wouldn't change things.

But it did. Didn't it?
Sure I still talked to him
        but only when *he* called.
        And I was always so eager
                to fill our conversations
                with my stories.
I did that, of course,
        so I wouldn't have to hear about his.
I never took the time
        to ask him
                how he was
                or what he did
                or who his friends were.

A virus killed my brother.
        But I did, too,
                by my distance,
                my silence,
                and the barriers I set up
                        to keep myself ignorant
                        of his sexuality.
I didn't want to know him
        and I have to live with that
        for the rest of my life.

I see all these friends of Matt's tonight,
        people who gave him
                the support
                and the love
                      that I never did.

What happened to us?
        We used to be so close,
                Matt and I.
It seems only yesterday
        I was pushing him
                on the merry-go-round
                    and helping him
                      learn to ride his bike.
I thought I was a good sister
        to him then,
        his friend.
But somewhere along the line we grew up

and we stopped being friends.

Tonight, I realize
        I'll never have the chance
                to change that.
I'll never have the chance
        to be the sister
        he wanted me to be,
                the sister
                he needed me to be.
And I'll never
        have the chance
        to know him.
I'll never know him
        as well as these friends of his,
                these strangers.

Part Six

# Money and the
# Modern Catholic

# Reflection

## Radical Hospitality:
## Forming a Lifestyle
## That Embraces the Gospel

The Gospel does not call us
    to poverty,
        at least,
            not if we understand poverty
                as destitution.
We are bound to eradicate poverty
    of that sort
    and establish a new order in our society
    in which destitution has no place
        whatsoever.
The kind of material poverty
    we know today
    around the world
        is evil.
It is a work of darkness
    and selfishness
    and greed.
And it is the radical call of all
    who follow Jesus
    to establish a lifestyle of justice
        in order to change that.
We've spent a lot of time
    so far in this book
    talking about other personal matters
        of sexuality,
        family life,
        prayer,
        and conscience.
But no where does the Gospel
    make itself more plain
    than in regard to money.
And this is the last thing

any of us want to hear,
any of us, at least,
who have a little money.
But we really don't have a complete ethic
of love and life,
until we do this.
So hang on
because this is going to be
a rough ride
for many of us.

Money is power
in our day and age;
there's no hiding that.
Money talks.
Money buys big houses and cars,
abundant food,
fashionable clothing,
electronic toys,
island vacations.
It buys more, more, more.
It's how we satisfy our hunger
when intimacy won't do
or we won't let it do.
All of us keep a mental list
of things we want
as soon as we get the money,
or the credit limit,
to buy it.
That little mental list
is our guide
and sometimes our god.

We would be blind not to see this
within and around us
and in a sense, we are blind.
In a sense, we don't see this.
We have become so accustomed
to pursuing this
as an "ultimate goal" in life
that we have forgotten
we are its slaves.
Like the Hebrew people

with the golden calf
which they worshipped
at the foot of the mountain,
we, too, worship what glitters.

Even the materially poor long for this
every day,
struggling to get rich.
And who can blame them?
Who would ever struggle
to become poor!?
Yet, "blessed are the poor...."
What does this mean?
...what does it mean for us?

I think we could lay down some principles
for thinking about money
as Catholic Christians
and we will begin this
by looking at the teachings
of Jesus himself.
The Gospels, of course,
give no blueprint;
they aren't an economics textbook.
But they do give us some hints
about how the ethic of Jesus
might be applied
to our modern lives.
Let's start with Matthew's Gospel.

Michael Crosby has given a pithy analysis
of this Gospel
in his *House of Disciples.*
When we read about Jesus' birth
in Matthew
we find there are no poor shepherds
guarding their flocks by night
and coming in haste to a stable.
Rather, Matthew presents us with
something more radical:
wealthy foreign visitors,
the Magi.
Traditionally we think of these Magi

as three men,
often called three kings,
            but the text of Matthew
            gives neither number nor gender.
The best we can surmise about them
            was that they were holy men or women,
            shamans, perhaps, from distant cultures:
                        wisdom figures
                        or healers.
They were persons
            in search of the abiding human truth
            about life, love, and longing.


And what did they do
            when they met Jesus?
They *shared their wealth*
            in *lavish* style,
            setting a pace for Matthew
                        that continued to the end
                        of this Gospel.
Later on, in chapter 26,
            a woman looks for and finds Jesus
            in the home of Simon the leper.
There she anoints him
            with "the most expensive ointment...."
When others object,
            Jesus defends her
            for she had offered a religious act
                        of love and devotion
                        to him.
But she had also engaged
            in an economic act:
            "Nothing should be spared
                        when caring for the Body of Christ."
                        Nothing.
This woman radically lavished herself
            and her wealth
            on others.
And at the end of this Gospel
            Jesus is buried
            by a "rich man from Arimathea...."
This man named Joseph
            was also a disciple of Jesus

but still maintained his wealth.
Throughout this Gospel
        it seems clear to us
        that apparently material poverty
        was not the goal for Jesus' followers.
Nowhere, Crosby has pointed out,
        do we read that either the disciples
                or Jesus
                were particularly poor.
Destitution is not the aim
        of the Gospel.
Something more demanding is.


Because once they met Jesus,
        something did change for people.
It wasn't that they became
        materially impoverished;
        it isn't that suddenly the world
                and clothing and food
                or housing and transportation
                or education and entertainment
                or gifts and vacations and money
                        become evil.
The world is not evil but good,
        created and good.
But for those who meet Jesus,
        there is a clear and definite shift
                in attitude.
Now, rather than hoarding selfishly,
        taking care of myself first,
        providing only for my own family,
        ignoring the plight of
                widows,
                orphans
                and strangers,
                        there is a new attitude.
The new attitude is characterized
        by love and openness,
                generosity,
                absolute readiness to place everything
                        at the disposal
                        of the New Community:
                        the Reign of God in Jesus Christ.

In a word,
>        once we meet Jesus
>        we take on the call to
>        *Radical Hospitality!*

So Joseph, the "rich man of Arimathea,"
>        like the magi before him
>        and the woman between them,
>                shared his resources generously
>                with the Body of Christ.
For us who follow Jesus
>        the call is no less.
It isn't a question, then,
>        of how we should become poor
>                but how we should re-order
>                        our lives,
>                        our homes,
>                        and our checkbooks.
"Re-order your lives!"
>        "Prepare the way of the Lord!"
>        "Repent and be saved!"
John the Baptist announced this new order
>        and called first-century folks
>                to conversion within it.

The very first words
>        from the mouth of Jesus
>        in this Gospel
>        make this all very plain for us as well.
He is about to be baptized by John
>        who objects,
>        saying that Jesus should baptize him instead.
Jesus refuses and he lays down
>        a principle
>        that will be repeated in this Gospel
>                seven times.
It can be translated in various ways
>        and might be rendered like this:
>        "We must do what God wants!"
>        "It is proper to do
>                what righteousness demands!"
>        "Let us set things in their right order."
>        "Justice demands right ordering of life."

For everyone who was close to him,
  their lives were re-ordered, too.
    And with their lives,
      their finances!
The closer you get to the experience of God,
  the more you want to share
  what you have,
    the more you want to change the system
    that makes some have so little.
The closer you get to Jesus,
  the more you want right ordering
  of the world,
    including its economics.
The closer you get to the Divine Lover,
  the more you want to open your hearts
    yourselves,
    the more you want to live
      in the New Community
      of Jesus Christ.
In Matthew, then,
  "Blessed are the poor" becomes
    "Blessed are the poor *in spirit...*"
  and "Blessed are they
    who hunger and thirst" becomes
    "Blessed are the ones
      who hunger and thirst
      *for right ordering!*"


Michael Crosby leads us to understand
  that this right ordering
  begins at home!
It's our households,
  literally our households
  that are to be ordered
    according to God's plan.
We are called to conversion,
  to a turning away from false gods
  and a turning to the Divine Force
    known in Jesus
    and now known within and among us.
This turning occurs for us
  in our everyday lives
  and while it is deeply personal

and profoundly unique to us
it is never private.
It is never private
which means we experience conversion
in the context of the New Community
in which we are now called to live.
And that New Community of Jesus
meets first in our homes
no matter where or how we live.


We are called to seek
"the pearl of great price"
rather than the glitter of gold.
We are called to sweep out our houses,
our households,
and make of them a home where God
can dwell.
It is a "hidden treasure"
for which we are called to look
and, when we find it,
to allow it to shape us.
This treasure is the Word
spoken in our lives,
bringing us home.
True wealth, we are told,
"is not stored in barns"
but in our hearts.
Right relationships are the mark
of the Reign of God
but it would be easier
"to pass a camel through a needle's eye
than for someone with unconverted wealth
to live in right relationships."
The rich young man
who came to Jesus asking guidance
wanted so much
but was willing to pay
so little.
All Jesus asked of him
was a new order for his finances,
a new arrangement of priorities
at home.
We are called, like him,

not to legal rigorism
or even to creeds of faith,
but to re-order our households
and to make everything we have
available to the Body of Christ.

What does this mean for us?
How can we do it?
How can we re-order our households?
It really isn't so terribly complex
but it is very challenging.

Let's invite our friends and family,
into our homes
but also strangers and the sick,
waifs and wanderers,
foreigners and passersby.
Let's make our households
into small communities of folks
gathered in solidarity,
bound together by the Spirit,
and sharing wealth.
Let's gather for meals,
for prayer,
for blessing unions and couples,
for support in conversion,
for discernment,
for a home to the world,
for strength in work for justice,
for a source of life
and a destiny as well.
It won't be a matter of *giving up* our homes
but of *opening up* our doors!

Once we begin to welcome everyone
to the banquet:
the refugees,
the impoverished,
and the imprisoned,
the lepers,
the sinners,
and the outcasts,
we will recognize within ourselves

our own sinfulness,
and our own impoverishment.
Then if we are poor,
we will become rich
and if we are rich,
we will give away our wealth.
We will learn how to dine with others,
how to share money,
how to accept without exclusion,
how to become stable,
permanent,
and faithful households of faith.
We will share life
so that sharing with the wider church
can be an expression of a reality
already present
and still being formed.
We will be satisfied at last,
stop wanting always "more."
The mental list we keep
will not be of possessions to buy
but of people to invite
to dinner.

Make no mistake about this,
if we are radical Christians
and if we have learned the ethics
of the Gospel
which are evident to all,
our lives will change.
But not just our lives,
our households as well,
the very roots of our life:
...where we live.
We will find
it isn't simply a matter of giving away
our dollars
or pounds
or pesos
but a matter of giving away
our hearts that counts.
So let's re-order our appointment books
to make the time for this again.

Let's re-order our checkbooks
       to afford a more generous sharing,
       no matter how little
           or how much
           we may have.
Let's re-order our attitudes toward people
       to love them unconditionally
       and make them really welcome.
Let's re-order our home lives
       to expect disruptions of this kind.
       We are so cautious,
           so afraid to risk sharing,
           so filled with "practical" needs
               and dull, routine habits.
Caution is the enemy of the Spirit
       and, if we are to open ourselves,
       we must expect a parade of unexpected,
           and uncontrollable folks
           to come marching through.
Let's open to that!
       It isn't possible to both live in the Spirit
       and also be in complete charge of your life!
There is no opportunity
       that isn't at the same time
       a potential danger
           but it's precisely these
           "dangerous opportunities"
           that will bring us to the doorstep
               of the Gospel.
What do you think Jesus was up to?
       Do you think safety and caution
           were his theme?

You probably think I'm suggesting
       that you take some of your savings,
       (even some of your retirement fund!)
           and throw a party or two
           a banquet for friends and strangers!
You probably think I'm suggesting
       that you watch less television
       and more of life itself.
You probably think I'm urging you
       to wear lavender shirts sometimes,

or to worry less about how you look,
or to suck more fully
        from the breasts of life!
You probably think I'm suggesting
        that, if you're rich
        you give away much of what you have
                and if you're poor,
                you call insistently for justice.
You probably think I'm suggesting
        that you take an inventory of your life
        (and your stuff!)
                and get a firm hold
                on your real desires,
                        to love,
                        to love well,
                        and to love deeply.
You probably even think I'm suggesting
        that we take Jesus seriously
        and "give what we have to the poor"
                so we can follow his truth
                and thus be able
                        to speak our own truths loudly.

And you're damn right.
        That's exactly
        what I'm suggesting.

# Comparing Our Ethic on Sex
# to Our Ethic on Greed

If I were to describe someone to you
        I thought was of "loose values"
            what kind of person
            would you imagine me
            to be talking about?
How do we measure "loose values"
        these days?
When we speak of someone who's
        "living in sin,"
        what do we usually mean?
Do we think of greed first?
        Would we say that greedy people
            are "living in sin?"
If I told you we were bringing someone up
        on a "morals charge,"
        what would you think I was talking about?
Would your first thought be
        "Oh, they caught another bomb-builder!"
Probably not. You'd think first
        of sexual impropriety.
        A "morals charge" is a sexual charge.

We are thoroughly convinced
        that sexual ethics
        are nearly the only "real" ethics
        with which individuals must be concerned.
We've elevated
        our rules about certain sexual issues
        to a place of near idolatry
        and ignored other very important matters
            at great social and personal cost.
Some church leaders see themselves
        as responsible for monitoring

         moral progress
            and keeping in check
            anyone who strays
                from the "company line."
But their pre-occupation seems to be with sex.

They nearly ignore, for example,
         the unbridled growth of capitalism,
         global warming,
         the collapse of the environment under our
            continual exploitation,
         the socio-political crises leading to
            war,
            famine,
            and wide-spread death
                across the developing world.
They nearly ignore
         the on-going exploitation of women
            around the world,
         the cruelty with which children are treated,
         the violence against gay men and lesbians,
            the homeless,
            and the weak.
They nearly ignore the AIDS epidemic
         because they judge those who have it
            morally weak
            and socially outcast.
They talk a lot about abortion.
         (They're against it,
         along with birth control.)
            But what about policymakers and voters
            opposed to prenatal care,
                job training programs,
                improved welfare benefits
                    for single mothers,
                day care,
                universal health insurance
                    and so on...?

The primary reason this over-emphasis
         on sexual ethics
         now dominates our churchly thinking
         must be the odd belief

that sexual ethics form the core
of Jesus' ethic!
Nothing could be
further from the truth!
Although he had plenty of ethical concerns,
Jesus rarely had anything to say
about sexual matters.
Most of Jesus' teachings had to do
with other important issues
of our day as well as his.
Jesus was possessed of a "whole person ethic,"
I think.
He was intent on forming a new community
where being a woman,
an outsider
a leper
a law breaker
a public sinner
a tax collector
or, we should presume,
a family on birth control
a gay man or a lesbian
a divorced or re-married person
indicated eligibility for membership.
Jesus was founding a new community
and calling these types first;
unconditionally calling them,
taking them into the Reign of God.
He was calling them to a new ethic,
a life of love,
and a spirit of generosity.
Why do you suppose he did that?
Why didn't he begin his work
with first-century church insiders:
their equivalent of today's
bishops and pastors?
I suspect his reasons were deeply intuitive,
deeply prayerful on his part.
In fact, the Gospel pictures him
going off to prayer
before choosing the friends he did.
I suspect he began with these,
the ones not quite in the mainstream

of church life,
        because he found them honest,
        because he found them whole.
He found them, I suspect,
        aware of their need for love
        and their need for him.
They listened to their hearts,
        trusted their human experience,
        and honestly admitted their own failures
            to be perfect.
Theirs was an inner guide,
        very much like Jesus' own relation
        to the one he calls "Abba."
I suspect he liked these
        and found in them a basis for his work
        because they, too, knew the struggle
            to hear God's voice
            in the din of other voices
                around them.
These people were full of passion
        because they were full of God's word
        spoken in the private silent place
            which is conscience.
The others,
        the church insiders,
        mistrusted this.
They preferred their laws,
        which weren't inner guides
            but outer ones.
But Jesus was insistent they were wrong;
        in fact,
        he often called the others,
        the church insiders,
            empty tombs.
"On the outside you look good,"
        he told them,
        "but inside you're empty
        because you keep the law
            but don't follow your own heart
            where I am waiting to meet you."

To me the most remarkable character
        in all the Gospels

is the woman, the sinful woman,
who found Jesus
in someone's rectory
and made her way to him,
weeping for her mistakes
but able at least to admit them....
Jesus called her a woman
full of great love,
even while the inhabitant of that rectory
found her repulsive.
Her sins were forgiven,
Jesus told her,
simply and soley
because of her great love!

He founded the new community
on that one principle: love.
The Law could be summed up and fulfilled
in that one saying of his:
"You shall love God above all,
and you shall love your neighbor
as yourself."

No doubt, he wanted lifestyles
where relationships were "right"
but he didn't have too much to say
about the role of sex in that.
In fact,
his teachings about right relations
showed far more concern
about our use of money
and here he had plenty to say.
As a result,
a great many of the moral sayings of Jesus
deal with money and wealth.
The Gospel of Matthew, for example,
opens with wealthy magi
sharing their gifts,
and closes with a rich man of Arimathea
sharing his tomb.
In between, there is a rich menu of moral sayings
and guidance on how to live
in the new community.

It has to do with sharing Earth
        and its wealth,
        with sharing ourselves in love,
        with sharing bread and wine
                when we gather,
        with sharing the burdens of the poor,
                the illness of the sick,
                the loneliness of the imprisoned.
The measure of the Reign of God
        in Matthew 25
        doesn't mention sexual ethics
        but places the focus squarely
                on other matters of lifestyle,
                ones we prefer not to hear about.
When the rich young man came to Jesus
        asking what is needed for life
        in the Reign of God,
                he wasn't asked to give up sex.
                He was asked to give up money.
We tend to ignore Jesus' moral focus here.

Most sexual activity is not evil,
        at least not as evil as greed,
        and church leaders who cling to sex
        as the primary moral concern of today
                appear ludicrous
                to anyone reading the Gospels.
We are left wondering how this narrow view
        of what is needed for the Reign of God
        can continue.
And by the thousands,
        Catholics and others
        have simply thrown up their hands
                in frustration.

It's time to move beyond
        this fixation on sexual ethics
        and tend to the larger questions
                of global concern
                and human need.
It's time to examine our conscience
        for "dirty thoughts"
        about having more money

        and bigger homes,
        and larger retirement funds
            while others starve.
Those are the real "dirty thoughts"
        we should be confessing.
It's time to examine our lives,
        and this includes the church itself,
        for hypocrisy in this regard.
When will we write our checks
        with the same fervor
        we do our Pastoral Letters?
When will we end the rationalizing
        that keeps us institutionally rich?
When will we recognize Jesus,
        really see him there!
        among the poor waiting for the rich
            to divest?

Our values are "loose," all right,
        but not because we're passionate
        about sex.
Our values are "loose" because
        we fail to embrace
        the ethic of Jesus
            and put our treasures
            where we want our hearts to be.

# A Young Man Reflects
# on a Stranger
# Who Had No Legs

I'm still thinking about him.
      Why can't I
      put him out of my mind?
He was there again tonight,
      sitting in his wheel chair,
      an African American man
           holding out an empty tin can.
           He had no legs.

The first time I saw him,
      I was out for a beer
      with some friends.
All I could see then
      was that he was black
         and poor
         and lame.
We were wrapping up
      a busy week at school,
      celebrating Friday.
Dressel's was our regular bar
      in the West End,
      a place to listen to some jazz
         and relax.
We were walking down the street
      admiring the beautiful homes
      when I saw him.
He was sitting patiently
      on the sidewalk,
      hoping those who walked by
         would drop some change
         into his soup can.

I passed him by
      that first time...

I simply passed him by.

But I saw him again tonight.
>        This time it was different.
>        I couldn't just casually walk
>                into the pub
>                and pretend he wasn't there.
So I put a few dollars
>        into his tin can
>                and went inside
>                with the rest of my friends.
We ordered a couple of Reubens
>        along with a side of chips
>        even though we'd just had a full dinner,
>        not more than three hours earlier.

We were sitting at a table,
>        piled high with food and beer,
>        the music playing loudly behind us,
>        chatter everywhere:
>                busy people,
>                busy lives,
>                busy bar.

But somehow I wasn't there;
>        something was missing for me,
>        I didn't know what.
Then it hit me:
>        it wasn't some*thing* that was missing
>        but some*one*,
>                that guy out on the street,
>                begging for his supper.
I couldn't shake the feeling,
>        almost a demand,
>        that he belonged in here with us.
He belonged to me,
>        just as these friends did.
Somehow, he was as much my brother
>        as my brother is my brother.

I thought about him
>        out on the street
>        and I wondered if he'd even had supper.

Or if he could afford
      to leave the street
      on this busy Friday night.
And I thought about the measly few dollars
      I'd placed into his can.
A ridiculous token:
      Did I really think that somehow it meant
      I'd done my duty to feed the hungry?
If I'd be willing to help
      my brothers and sisters
      related to me in blood,
            why is it then
            that I'm so hesitant
            to help my brothers and sisters
                  whom I know are related to me
                      in Christ?

How can I go on
      day after day
      and not change
      my current comfortable lifestyle?
I don't need to look toward Ethiopia
      to see the faces of the hungry.
            They're here in my midst.
Perhaps I'm only just beginning
      to be shocked
      out of my white, middle-class
          complacency.
Perhaps I'm the one
      who is really lame and poor;
      maybe I'm the one
         waiting to be helped.
Perhaps he's the one
      who'll help me see
      we really are brothers after all.

*Pause*

I fear the change in my life
      that I know must come.
But what I fear more
      is that I'll fall back
      into the safe,

       antiseptic world
       I've been living in.
I'm afraid I'll forget
       the first time I saw him
       and that I passed him by.
I simply passed him by.

# A Woman Wonders
# Why She Never
# Has Enough Money

Do you think I'm greedy?
     I'm actually not.
     At least I don't *think* I am.
       Not *really* greedy
       like some people are!
Something happened to me today
     though,
     to make me doubt myself.
Something happened
     I wasn't expecting.

I was reading my mail this morning
     and I got a letter
     from one of those agencies
       that sponsors kids
       in the Third World.
I get these all the time
     and I usually glance over them
     and toss them out.
In general, I think there are too many people
     begging for money
     these days.
     Too much junk mail, period.

But today, for some reason,
     I was caught by a story
     in one of these begging letters
       about a family in Guatemala.
The last name was Vasquez or something
     and they lived
     in a village called San Lucas.
       They were really poor.
I've heard about poverty sometimes
     that seemed really bad,

you know, families with no toys for Christmas,
a kid who can't afford surgery,
poor folks who live in the mountains.
But these people in Guatemala were really poor,
poor as you can imagine.


In the first place, they had no money,
and, in the second,
they had a terrible house,
built out of corn stalks.
Imagine that! A corn stalk house!
What would you do if it rained?
It had a tin roof
and only one room
and they all had to sleep together
...sort of.
This is really awful of me
but I wondered as I read this
how the parents could have sex
with all those kids
right next to them there.
I mean, they couldn't have much privacy,
I wouldn't think.
But they must have figured it out
because they had a bunch of kids,
most of them sick.
Two or three had already died
and I felt real bad about that.
The letter included a picture of their house
and I couldn't believe it.
It was so small
and crowded.
The only running water was a pipe
sticking up from the ground
out on their lawn.
Well, you couldn't really call it a *lawn*,
it didn't have any actual grass;
mostly just dirt
and tree branches.
The water pipe just stuck up from the ground,
and I guess anytime they needed water
they'd just have to go out there
to get some.

I don't suppose they had a toilet.
>There must have been an outhouse
>>or something.
The father in this family
>actually had a job.
>He picked coffee every day
>>for a plantation
>>and the coffee was shipped to England
>>>or somewhere.
Now this is the part I just couldn't believe:
>He got paid only three dollars per day!
>>Three dollars!
How could they live on three dollars?!
>>So much for the poetic coffee commercials
>>of Juan Valdez and his donkey!
There was a photo of the family
>showing the mom and dad
>and four little kids
>>all standing in front
>>of that little corn stalk house.
Looking at their faces,
>I felt really bad for them
>and I decided to send them a check,
>>maybe twenty dollars or something,
>>to help them out a little.
But then I got to thinking,
>maybe twenty dollars isn't enough,
>maybe I should send a little more.
So I made it for fifty
>and sent it right then and there
>and I felt a lot better after that....

A couple hours later, though
>I changed my mind
>but it was too late to retrieve it
>>from the mailbox.
I wanted my money back.
>Fifty bucks is a lot of money these days
>and I decided I could use it better
>>if I just kept it here.
What good would fifty lousy bucks do
>in Guatemala anyway?
But it was too late

and off my money went.
I'll never see it again.

Now tonight I'm wondering
        about all this.
I think I was taken in by a smooth operator
        begging for money
        and using my guilt to get it.
These people were probably an exception,
        maybe even posed for the picture
        in old clothes or something.
They probably aren't really as poor
        as the letter said.
                These missionary types, you know,
                you really can't always trust them.

We really don't have that much stuff here,
        not when you stop to think about it.
We really aren't *that* rich,
        not that much better off than others.
We do have a nice house
        but we also have two kids
        and their friends coming over all the time.
And we have the car,
        well actually,
        we have two cars,
                one for John (my husband)
                and mine.
I drive a cute little Jeep,
        four doors,
        very practical.
And John has his Mercury;
        he's always liked a Mercury.
And then we do have new furniture this year
        but the old stuff was really bad,
        almost eight years old,
                my God,
                and I hated the color.
When I bought it everyone was buying green
        but no one has green furniture
        these days.
John insisted we get new carpet right away,
        since the old rug really was worn,

especially by the door.
But that's it;
    that's all we did to the house
    this whole year.
That isn't so bad, is it?


And we had a very small Christmas
    this year.
We had the usual gifts for the kids,
    toys and clothes and such,
    but nothing big,
        though I must admit
        the pile under the tree always gets bigger
        than I want it to.
And instead of going to the islands this winter,
    John and I are only taking a cruise,
    and only for one week.
We're saving almost a thousand dollars
    that way
    and times are a little tight.
We try to save a little
    wherever we can
    and this year it's our vacation
        we cut back on.
But, of course,
    we do still have the cottage "up north."
    You can't really blame us
        for hanging on to that.
        We got such a steal when we bought it
        and it'd be a shame to let it go.


What really disturbs me
    is how we never seem to have
        enough money.
That's why sending that fifty bucks
    hurt so much today.
I don't know where all our money goes
    but we always seem to be
    a little short.
There're dance lessons to pay for one week,
    piano lessons the next.
Then, of course,
    there're the boat payments;

we do have a boat but everyone has a boat
these days
and it wouldn't make any sense
to have a lake cottage
if we didn't have a boat to enjoy it with,
would it?
John needs new suits
and I like to have new outfits
for my job.
I've been working as an attorney
since 1978
so you can just imagine
how much clothes that takes!
And we always have our parish
begging for money.
Half the people who belong to our church
don't show up
and don't contribute
so we end up supporting them, too.
It doesn't seem very fair
but we do it week after week.

So you see?
The money just slips away
and we never seem to have quite enough,
even with both of us working
and only two kids.
We have a lot of priorities,
lots of commitments
and it bothers me when these poor people
come along and think we should give them
our hard-earned cash.
Let them get jobs of their own!

And I think it's just terrible
how they use guilt
to try to get us to give.
It isn't fair to compare our lifestyles,
or homes,
or children.
God has blessed us
by giving us what we have
and they have what they have

and that's not really our problem.

If God didn't want us to keep what we have,
        then why did he give it to us
        in the first place?
I don't believe Jesus expects us
        to take care of every
        Tom, Dick, and Harry who comes along
                with a hand out,
                not to mention Jose, Maria, or Carlos!
Maybe I'm prejudiced
        but it just seems
        that all the poor people
                are foreigners, besides.
They just can't understand
        what it takes to live in the USA
        and, even if they did,
                where would they live?

Does my rambling on like this
        bother you?
I'm sorry.
        It's just that I just sent fifty
        of my hard-earned bucks
        off to sponsor some kid in the third world
                and I can hardly support my own
                right here at home!
And even though I sent the money,
        I still feel greedy
        and I don't like it.
*They* made me feel that way
        and it's not fair!

It's just not fair.

# Epilogue

# Taking Bread and Wine (and Feet!)
# Into Our Own Hands

## Reflection
In this guide,
> we have spent considerable
> time and effort
>> learning to take back into our own hands
>> the responsibility for choosing
>> how to live in these modern times.

We have considered the place of discernment,
> Sacred Scripture
> official church teachings,
> and, above all,
>> our own LifeSongs of faith.

We have found ways to validate
> and legitimate our decisions
> made in good conscience
>> and we have challenged ourselves
>> to join with one another
>> in radical community.

It is in gathering together
> and sharing vision and story,
> sharing scripture and witness,
>> that we find our truest way.

The Gospels present Jesus
> as teacher and healer
> but they present him first and foremost
>> as part of a small community.

It wasn't a perfect community
> (one of them finally turned him in!),
> but it was where they lived,
>> and ate,
>> and grew together.

It's where they learned about prayer
> and personal sacrifice,
> about dying and rising,
> about truth and beauty and light.

Their stories
    are our stories, too,
    and what Jesus asked of them
        he also asks of us.
Now that we have learned
    to take into our own hands
    the responsibility for our lives,
        let's take into our hands as well
        the story of Jesus,
            especially the *Great* story!

In each of the Gospels,
    Jesus is pictured
    having dinner with his friends
    on the night before he died.
We easily can see this is no common meal.
    It was a special dinner,
        one that would be his last,
        one that his followers would remember
            forever....
It was a community, evening meal,
    taking its time,
    being a chance for them to talk together
        as they'd done so many times before.
But this time it was different;
    there was a "warning" in the air:
        Jesus was in deep trouble now
        with church authority
            and there seemed no further escape
            from them.
Let's put this in modern,
    rather than first-century, terms:
        Exactly what would happen to Jesus
        seemed uncertain,
        but one thing was clear:
        the local bishop was angry!

Matthew, Mark, and Luke tell the story
    of this meal
    with very similar words.
Jesus took bread during the meal,
    which was a long-standing Jewish custom,
    and shared it as a blessing

with them all.
And he took a cup,
        filled it with wine,
                and shared it, too.
This was the Elijah cup,
        the cup reserved on
        for the one who was to come.
Eating from one loaf,
        drinking from one cup:
        these were great signs of solidarity,
                unity,
                inclusivity,
                standing together,
                being at one.
The act of eating and drinking this way
        both celebrated what they already experienced:
                love,
                commitment,
                and joy in being together;
                        as well as helped deepen
                        those bonds.
This simple custom of the Jews
        with simple, everyday things:
        bread and wine,
        was very powerful for them.

Certainly it wasn't the first time
        they'd done this
        and for Jesus' followers
                it would not be the last.
Sitting at table together,
        sharing,
        laughing,
        delighting in one another
                would go on for them.
And because of this night,
        this unique night,
        when they repeated that old custom
        of taking bread and wine
                as a blessing,
                they would do it now
                in memory of Jesus.
And so they did...

...but do we do that today?

Oh, I know we offer weekend and daily Masses
    in most of our churches
    most of the time.
But do we really do
    what Jesus and his friends did?
There's a strong tendency
    on the part of many Christians today,
    to attend weekend worship
        with less energy and enthusiasm
        than we see at most ball games.
It isn't at all the same
    as those first-century Jews
    sitting down to that meal together.
Our goal certainly is not
    to reproduce that event
    in dramatic form.
Our goal isn't to play act
    the "Last Supper...."
What we do want, though
    is to recapture that spirit,
        no doubt!
We want our Eucharist
    to have at its center,
    the same spirit that was at the center
        of Jesus' own community meal.

Can we say of our own churches
    that the spirit of the Lord's Supper
    is present when we assemble there?
Can we see in one another
    what Jesus and his friends
    saw in each other?
Can we look into one another's eyes at Mass
    and find there a sister or brother?
After celebrating Mass together,
    which is both a joyful
        and a painful
        thing to do,
        could we have the courage
            to go to the Cross?

We need our assemblies on weekends,
        where we celebrate the Mass.
    We need their energy and
            their social-awareness-raising;
                we need to meet one another as friends
                and we need to meet
                        the strangers among us.
We need to gather with our priests
        and other ministers
        and each other to break bread
                on that huge table of life
                and to share the Elijah cup
                        passed to us
                        by Jesus himself.


But we also need to gather
        as households
        or small communities.
We also need the intimacy and challenge,
        the honesty and warmth,
        the spirit and love
                which only a household
                or small community can offer.
We need to gather away from the church buildings
        to witness to one another and the world
                about our commitment
                to the Body of Christ.
In short,
        we also need eucharist at home.


Of course,
        we already have it.
Many people already have begun
        to take the bread and the cup
        into their own hands
                and celebrate together.
Many women's groups,
        especially,
        are leading the way in this regard.


But why is it,
        do you think,
        that most Christians,

and most Catholics in particular,
        are "afraid" of doing this?
Why do you think
        we so seldom take bread and wine
        —or feet!
        and do with them what Jesus
                is said to have done?
Why are we hesitant
        to take bread,
        bless it and share it
                with family, friends, and colleagues?
Why are we reluctant
        to make sacramental
        our own household meals,
        the daily table at which we sit,
                not to mention
                the celebration tables
                        of our holidays
                        birthdays
                        Sundays
                        and anniversaries?
Why do we confine to the churches
        what we ourselves can do?


I suspect the answer to these questions
        and what that answer means
        will sound and feel
        sacriligious to many readers.
We all know in our bones
        why we personally are so reluctant
        to take bread and wine,
                to break it
                to share the common cup
        and so to bless ourselves and each other.
The first reason we are so reluctant
        is because we think
                it would be wrong.


Listen to the sound
        of that answer again:
We do not,
        on our own,
        follow the very example

which Jesus urged us to
because we think it would be wrong!

Wrong?
Do we think it would be wrong
       to give thanks,
       to offer eucharist
           in our homes?
Do we think it would be wrong
       to invite our families
           or friends
           or lovers
           to share this holy act with us?
The word eucharist is Greek in its origin
       and it means
       "thanksgiving."
It's customarily done in the context of a meal
       as a way of making gratitude clear,
       a way of ritualizing it.
We have loaded this word up
       with other meanings,
           however.
One of them has to do with our belief
       that we can't do this
       without a priest or minister
       present and in charge.
Our belief is
       that only the presence of clergy
       can make the "real presence" real.
Eucharist means
       "something we do with clergy present."
       It's one of the meanings we assign
           to this great, holy act.
It wouldn't be "valid"
       without an ordained person present.
       It would not, in short,
           be legal.

Let's pause to consider this
       before moving on.
Without getting into the technical question
       of Real Presence
       for a moment here,

                    let's consider
                    what this reluctance means.
I believe this great, holy act
          of breaking bread
          and sharing a common cup
                    forms the church.
It forms the way we feel and think
          about each other
          but, most importantly,
          it can place our focus squarely
                    on the real Body of Christ:
                    the ones mentioned in Matthew 25,
                    the ones on the margins,
                    the sinners and outcasts,
                              even our own sinning
                              and outcasting.
It's pretty tough to read Jesus' story
          and mimic his behavior
          without being confronted by this.
Like it or not,
          Jesus took us in:
                    all of us
                    as part of his body.
And that includes the messiness of life
          the outrageous
          and the least desirable among us.
Jesus took us all in
          and eucharist is a thanksgiving for that,
          for having been accepted and loved
                    unconditionally,
                    forever,
                              and ever....
So, doing this together
          is powerful:
          it can change our lives.
And if we lived in the early church
          we would have less hesitation
          about naming our own leaders.
We would be more courageous
          about taking this into our own hands
          and more insistent about the bread.
For when we gather
          in the name of Jesus

to form the New Community in him,
        can we really remember him
        without this?
Can we ever develop meaningful, profound
        and holy bonds
        unless this story is told
                again and again and again....

But there's another reason
        we don't do it.
Celebrating eucharist at home
        which seems easy and fun at first,
        is really very difficult
                because it's such a risk.
It's a terrible risk
        to look across the table at someone
        and say to him or her,
                or to them:

        "Do we have or do we want
                Jesus at our center
                with the solidarity that implies?"
        "Do we or can we come to love each other
                        this much?"
        "Are we or can we be this committed?"
        "Will we really receive the Body of Christ,
                with all its bruises
                        and imperfections,
                        and needs?
                all its unwanted
                        unwashed
                        and unhealed?"
        "Are we really ready for this?"

These are very intimate questions
        because they put us on the line
        with the people
                at our own table,
                the ones with whom we break bread,
                our "Companions."
And they put us on the line
        with those others:
                the ones in Matthew 25,

the ones on the margins,
the ones we dislike
or disown
or dispossess.
It is our tools
that determine our trade in life
and the tools of eucharist
are a towel and basin.
In the Gospel of John
the bread, if there was any,
is not mentioned at all.
The writer of that Gospel was able to sum up
all that eucharist means
without the food;
all that was needed to tell the story
was that towel and basin.
We read this story at Mass
only on one evening in the entire year:
Holy Thursday,
when very few people can be present.
I think that's a great shame
because it's really the charter document
of the church,
of our households,
and of our small communities.
The point made here
is that if we have not washed
one another's feet
with a life of service
to the body of Christ,
the community present and absent,
then we really haven't *received*
communion.
But it isn't easy
to be so intimate
and to risk this much faith.
It's much easier
to just go to Mass on Sunday
which involves almost no risk at all
in much of the modern world.

It seems sad that Christians
are so afraid of taking bread themselves

and blessing it
       and entering into a life
       of community.
But if Christians
       are afraid to take bread
       into their own hands,
              they are even more afraid
              to take the Word.
The base communities of Latin America
       have overcome this fear;
       they have taken the Scripture
              and consumed it,
              internalized it,
              broken it open in their lives.
It turned out,
       without their planning it this way,
       that this Word of God
              was *revolutionary.*
They should have known
       because if you know the story,
       you know that Jesus turned
              the customs and culture of his time
              into a heap.
His ethic,
       which is to say,
       "his way of living in the world,"
       was indeed revolutionary.
As I have argued here already so often,
       the law, according to Jesus,
       is not sufficient to save anyone.
But the condition of the heart,
       the place of love,
       justice,
       charity,
       and compassion can indeed save.
Jesus came to transform the world
       by transforming the human heart
              in love.
Revolutionary.

As a result
       of his unconditonal acceptance and love
       Jesus and his way of living

will be a scandal to many,
            to *many!*
We don't understand this very well,
            we modern Christians,
            because we don't break open the Word
                        at home.
We don't let the Scriptures
            develop in us,
            grow and mature in us,
            and change us.
Like bread and wine,
            and one another's feet,
            we don't take it into our own hands
                        very often.

Let's change all this!
            Let's take the Word at home
            and read it,
            break it open,
            share it among ourselves,
            let it empower us,
                        lead us,
                        fill us with its spirit.
And let's take bread
            as Jesus did,
            and tell again the story of his life
                        and his mission to transform the world,
                        and then share it.
Let's take real bread,
            a loaf from the kitchen,
            regardless the recipe.
Bread out of life,
            bread that tomorrow will be breakfast
                        for us.
We should save the crusts for this.
            Crusts can be especially symbolic,
                        I think.
Or let's take pita,
            or corn tortilla:
            whatever we normally eat as bread.

Then let's take the cup,
            the kind we drink from every day,

and fill it,
          *fill it* with wine.
It needn't be choice wine
          because we don't usually drink
                    such choice wines.
Really, any old common wine
          will do just fine,
          a wine from our life
                    and the lives of those around us.


Let the Word
          be a light to our lives.
Let the bread be a symbol
          of the Body of Christ
          for which we have committed our lives.
And when we take the bread,
          and pass it to each other
          let's gaze into each other's eyes
                    and call each other
                    to consume
                    and internalize
                    and be nourished by this Great Body,
                              the Body of Christ.
But let's also call each other
          to take care to love
          the whole Body of Christ as well.
And when we have eaten,
          let's pass the one cup
          and let it be a sign of the solidarity
                    we need for this work
                    and receive in the energy of Christ.
Let's pass the Elijah cup
          as Christ did,
          inviting one another to Messianic lives,
                    in this Messianic age.
And once we've taken
          the word
          and the bread
          and the Elijah cup
                    into our own hands,
                    let's take one another's feet next!
Let's serve one another now
          from the spiritual bonds we share

and let's change the world
for Christ.
Let's wash the feet of the world,
the tired aching feet of Guatemalan Mayans,
the trimmed and pedicured feet of Madison Avenue,
the busy feet of parents,
the tiny feet of children around the world,
the determined feet of women today,
the feet in army boots carrying guns and bombs,
those in the shoes of priests,
neighbors,
homeless,
or hopeless people everywhere.
Let's make a pact with each other,
a covenant,
that we will stay together
until the feet of the world
march together on the Mountain of Justice.


Now I realize that all this
might not be technically valid,
but there might be a chance
for "real presence" regardless.
It might be meaningful in other ways
even if it isn't so meaningful
in the legal sense.
It might capture the Spirit
of the Lord's Supper.
The Word might be shared
simply,
roughly,
uncertainly.
The bread might be made
from some "inappropriate" recipe,
not approved for this.
There might not be many controls
on what goes on at the table
if the table were in our dining rooms.
We might not be able to control who will preside,
who will say what words,
when to kneel and when to stand,
who can share and who can't,
how to exclude those "not worthy"

of eucharist:
remarried folks,
non-Catholics,
sinners,
            and the like....
The wine we use might come from the bottle
        we just drank for dinner,
        I realize.
It might be common, ordinary wine,
        nothing especially "sacramental,"
            I know.


But despite these risks,
        I can tell you safely
        this is a powerful, real act.
It is a deeply sacramental act.
It is a revolutionary act.


Rather than adding priests
        so we can have more weekend Masses,
        maybe we should simply and solemnly
        guide one another
            to the Body of Christ
            at home.
Then when we gather together
        in our churches
        on Sunday mornings
            we would be there
            as people invested in that Rite.
Then the symbol of that one bread
        and one cup
        would take on powerful new meanings.
We would come to that larger community table
        differently
                if we came as members already
                of a celebrating community.


So let's gather as households or communities
        in our homes for simple, elegant meals.
Let's include those we might not immediately
        remember or want with us....
Let's invite those with whom we
        hope to reconcile,

those who might not otherwise eat,
    those who might eat alone.
At other times,
    let's just be together ourselves:
        friends and lovers,
        families and neighbors,
        small communities and households.


Let's serve simple foods
    but serve them with some elegance
    and not be afraid to light a candle
        on the table
        now and then.
Then after the meal,
    let's just push back the dishes
    and take some time to remember
    the Lord's Supper.
First, tell the story in simple words:
    Jesus gathered like this one night
    with his friends and lovers.
    Those who feared him wanted to kill him
    but he avoided them long enough
    to share one last meal with those he loved.
    During their meal he took bread
    into his own hands.
    He blessed it, breaking it as a symbol
    of his own body about to be broken, too.
    He gave them the bread to eat
    and they all shared it among themselves.
    Then he took into his own hands
    the Elijah cup, reserved for the one to come,
    but rather than drinking it alone
    he passed it to them
    as he now passes it to us
    and invited us all to drink of this mission,
    invited us all to share this baptism.
    Then he rose from the table
    and took off his outer garment,
    replacing it with an apron.
    He took a basin filled with water
    and a towel
    and one by one washed the feet of his friends,
    saying to them:

"Do you know what I have done to you?
I am your teacher and friend
and I have washed your feet.
You should do now for one another
what you have seen me do for you.
And whenever you are together like this,
remember me.
Tell this story forever
and I will be present in your midst."

After re-telling this story,
    for the countless-millionth time
    from its beginning until now,
        let's pause for a moment
        before sharing the bread and cup,
        to pray.
Let's call to mind in prayer those
    who are part of the Body of Christ
    and those who are not.
Let's be lovingly present to all whose lives
    are touched by us
    as well as those whose lives are not.
Let's pray that the christic energy
    we share here
    may reach into the darkness
        around us
        and heal,
            and reconcile,
            and enlighten it all!

Then let's simply take bread from the plate
    and pour a common cup of wine
        to share!

Let silence follow
    and fill us
    and our homes with its power.
Think about what we will have done:
    we'll have experienced
    a post-resurrection appearance
        of the Risen Lord.
We'll have recognized him
    in the breaking of the bread

just as the disciples did
in Emmaus.
We'll find
that we cannot miss him now
when we meet him in the streets:
among the homeless,
the sick,
the hungry,
the imprisoned,
the ones outside the church,
outside the rules,
outside the norms of culture.


What a way to end a meal
as a household
or small community of faith!
If it isn't a gathering for dinner
then let's simply place bread and wine
on the table in our center
and pray together
in gratitude and blessing.
If it is two of us,
it can be very simple;
when there are more,
let's adjust for them all.
If we're a small community,
let the leadership rotate
and the bread and wine be plentiful.
In our homes,
let the presider be the cook
if it is at table,
or the host if not.
And let our place of gathering vary,
moving from home to home,
blessing them all
in this powerful way.
Whenever we can
let's gather as well on Sundays
with the whole parish assembly
and there we'll find new energy
because of the energy we share.

At-home eucharist
      might point the way
      to the integration of the teachings
            of Jesus
            into ordinary life.
And I can assure you
      that Christ will seldom be
      more really present
            in our homes:
            among our family and friends,
            with our lovers and partners,
            or in our small communities
      than when we share bread and wine
      as part of our daily life.
This is the way
      to join the Revolution,
      the Christic Revolution,
            in our world.

# Resources
## to Enhance Your Discernment

*Embodiment: An Approach to Sexuality and Christian Theology*
James B. Nelson
Augsburg Press, Minneapolis, 1978.

*Catholicism*
Richard P. McBrien
Winston Press, Minneapolis, 1980.

*Moralilty and Its Beyond*
Dick Westley
Twenty-Third Publications, Mystic, Connecticut, 1984.

*In Pursuit of Love: Catholic Morality and Human Sexuality*
Vincent Genovesi
Michael Glazier, Collegeville, Minnesota, 1987.

*Catholic Morality Revisited: Origins and Contemporary Challenges*
Gerard Sloyan
Twenty-Third Publications, Mystic, Connecticut, 1990.

*Words Made Flesh*
Fran Ferder
Ave Maria Press, Notre Dame, Indiana, 1986.

*Intimacy and the Hungers of the Heart*
Pat Collins
Twenty-Third Publications, Mystic, Connecticut, 1991.

*A Theology of Presence: The Search for Meaning in the American Catholic Experience*
Dick Westley
Twenty-Third Publications, Mystic, Connecticut, 1988.

*Building Bridges: Gay and Lesbian Reality and the Catholic Church*
Robert Nugent and Jeannine Gramick
Twenty-Third Publications, Mystic, Connecticut, 1991.

*Constructing Gay Theology*
> Michael Stemmeler and J. Michael Clark, eds.
> Monument Press, Las Colinas, Texas, 1991.

*Dirt, Greed, and Sex*
> William Countryman
> Fortress Press, Minneapolis, 1988.

*House of Disciples*
> Michael Crosby
> Orbis Books, Maryknoll, New York, 1988.

*The Faith That Does Justice*
> John C. Haughey, ed.
> Paulist Press, New York, 1977.

*WomanWord*
> Miriam Therese Winter
> Crossroad, New York, 1990.

*A World at Prayer*
> Compiled by John Carden
> Twenty-Third Publications, Mystic, Connecticut, 1990.

*More Than Words*
> Janet Schaffran and Pat Kozak
> Crossroad, New York, 1991.

*The Rise of Christian Conscience*
> Jim Wallis, ed.
> Harper & Row, San Francisco, 1987.

*The Intimate Connection*
> James B. Nelson
> Westminster Press, Philadelphia, 1988.

*Your Sexual Self*
> Fran Ferder and John Heagle
> Ave Maria Press, Notre Dame, Indiana, 1992.

*Dangerous Memories*
> Bernard Lee and Michael Cowan
> Sheed & Ward, Kansas City, 1986.